Short Takes in Fiction

Critical Thinking, Reading, and Writing

Robert L. Saitz
Boston University

Francine B. Stieglitz
Boston University

Short Takes in Fiction

Critical Thinking, Reading, and Writing

Robert L. Saitz
Francine B. Stieglitz

 Addison-Wesley Publishing Company

Reading, Massachusetts · Menlo Park, California · New York
Don Mills, Ontario · Wokingham, England · Amsterdam · Bonn
Sydney · Singapore · Tokyo · Madrid · San Juan · Paris
Seoul · Milan · Mexico City · Taipei

A Publication of the ESL Publishing Group

Editorial
Karen Doyle, Kathleen Sands-Boehmer

Manufacturing/Production
James W. Gibbons

Text Design
Laura Fredericks

Cover Design
Marshall Henrichs

ISBN: 0-201-51677-2
4 5 6 7 8 9 10-CRS-99 98 97 96 95 94

Contents

Introduction

Short Takes in Fiction engages students in reading, speaking, and writing English through a content that concerns what is important in the lives of all of us: our feelings, of loneliness and of community; our relationships with others; our moments of freedom and insight; what challenges us, what fools us, and what amuses us. The text is arranged thematically into six units, and each reading is accompanied by a variety of exercises. It is especially designed for students at an intermediate level of proficiency.

The readings are short selections of original literature by twentieth century authors writing in English. For all readers, literature is rich. One of its distinguishing qualities is its insight as it focuses on what is significant in our lives by pulling important events, feelings, thoughts, and relationships out of time, where we often don't pay attention to them, and presenting them in a story, novel, or poem so that we do become aware. A second quality of literature is its power of giving pleasure. We expect students to find value in reading literature if the stories provide knowledge or pleasure or both. And we hope that people who read will become people who in turn will give pleasure, inform, and enhance their societies.

The readings in this text have therefore been chosen so that each short and fairly simple selection concerns itself with material that is at the same time familiar and new—with the universal relevance and multiple meaning of all good literature, well-written, and capable of stimulating thought and pleasure. To this end, we have selected readings from contemporary literature that deal with universal experiences seen through the visions of insightful authors.

The major focus is on personal experience, feelings, and thoughts with the expectation that students will react to the experiences described, relate them to their own lives and express their feelings and thoughts. The exercises that accompany each selection require students to observe, measure, reason, and speculate. It is anticipated that, with the aid of their instructors, they will not only use their language skills but will learn something about themselves, others, and the world.

The readings are brief, yet extensive enough to give the reader a feeling for the mind of the author and an understanding of the author's insight.

The authors are writers of significant stature, but many of these selections have not yet been anthologized. The language of the readings is the original language of the authors, but we have tried to avoid dialectal and exceptionally difficult prose. Some selections are more difficult than others so that instructors working at the lower end of the intermediate range can focus on the simpler readings while other instructors can focus on the more complex ones or follow the order in the text. For example, in Unit 1, the third selection, "Lucy," is more difficult than the others. Depending on the level of the class and the length of the course, instructors may choose to postpone or even eliminate that reading. The units are not sequenced in order of complexity; instructors may adopt any order they judge appropriate for the class, whether based on language level, subject interest, student background, etc. However, some questions in the later units may refer back to earlier readings.

The text has a variety of exercises accompanying the selections. These exercises include structural, communicative, investigative and creative/imaginative activities, all of which derive from the themes of the readings. As distinct from language activities which focus on text analysis, these activities use the text as a point of departure. The language that students are asked to produce in the exercises is, of course, at a significantly lower level than that of the readings although a number of exercises are open so that students may respond at their own levels of proficiency.

Each unit is preceded by the Unit Introduction, where the theme of the unit is set by having the students talk and/or write about their own experiences; the students thus invest their energy and build up a common background which serves as an introduction to the stories that follow. Each reading is preceded by a set of Pre-Reading questions; again these questions are directed to the students' experiences and they relate those experiences to the specific matter of the reading. After each reading, there is a glossary of idioms and new vocabulary. The language exercises then begin with two vocabulary activities: the first concentrates on key words, words that are particularly significant for the theme of the story and at the same time useful for vocabulary enhancement. These include "everyday" words (such as *accustomed to*) and words whose mastery gives students the sense that they are genuinely progressing through this intermediate level (such as *spoiled*). The second vocabulary exercise is a fill-in that includes the key words plus others from the reading with the cue sentences containing content from the reading. After the vocabulary exercises comes a comprehension exercise whose answers will appropriately use the words presented in the vocabulary exercises. The exercises following include a range of creative activities that focus on observation, recall, analysis, and the production of complex sentences. Many of these exercises can be done either orally or in writing. Instructors may find that, in doing the exercises orally first, discussion often stimulates the kinds of critical thinking that lead to better writing. The two final exercises offer suggestions for longer writing assignments and also serve as a basis for independent study assignments that take off from the content of the reading. The students are thus offered a variety of interactive speaking and writing activities that direct the students to pool their knowledge, brainstorm, and consult outside sources.

At the end of each unit there is a set of unit activities. These take advantage of the similarities and differences among the selections in the unit and stimulate students to think, talk and write about them. Some activities focus on the content of the readings, requiring students to compare and evaluate the experiences, i.e., to reason about them. Others introduce the possibility of role-playing, asking students to project themselves, or indicate why they might not want to project themselves, into the situations of the characters in the stories. A third type of activity encourages students to use their imaginations and view the theme from a new perspective.

It should be noted that there are a good number of exercises throughout the text, and it is not expected that all students will do all exercises. The instructor may select a core of exercises for the whole class, depending on class level, and assign others to small groups or to individuals for completion outside of class, or if possible during group work in class. If time is limited, the instructor may also choose to use only one or two of the three selections in each unit and allow the students to do the additional readings on their own.

We have enjoyed writing *Short Takes in Fiction*, and we hope that you will enjoy using it.

Robert L. Saitz
Francine B. Stieglitz

Preface to Students

This book is a collection of short readings in English which were written by twentieth-century authors. Most of the authors are contemporary, and all of them are considered good writers. They come from the United States, Great Britain, Canada, Australia, and India.

We chose these particular readings because we think that they are interesting and significant. The readings are about a variety of people, about how they think, how they feel, how they talk, and how they live.

The selections are not simplified. This means that some parts will be difficult. We have explained most of the idioms and difficult references, but we have not explained words that you can easily look up in a dictionary. Most of you will probably have to use a dictionary as you read these original selections, and we recommend an English-English dictionary such as *The Advanced Learner's Dictionary of Current English* by Hornby, Gatenby, and Wakefield or *The American Heritage Dictionary*.

We have also included language exercises that should encourage you to use English to say and write things about yourself, your ideas, your feelings, and your culture. We hope that you will enjoy both the readings and the exercises. We have enjoyed preparing them.

Short Takes in Fiction

in Fiction

Critical Thinking, Reading, and Writing

UNIT ONE — Exploring Differences

UNIT INTRODUCTION

The stories in Unit One focus on important changes in our lives: when we move to a different place or when we react in different ways from the ways of our parents. In the first story in this unit, Gopal, who is from India, is visiting France and is faced with the difficulty of adapting to a life very different from the life of his family. The second story deals with the different expectations of a mother born in China and her daughter who was born in the United States. In "Lucy," a girl from Jamaica has moved to the United States. She has left her family and she doesn't know what she is going to do with her life.

UNIT PRE-READING

1. Tell about how you felt, how you thought, or how you changed because of some event or change in your life. Some possibilities for topics are: moving to a new place; becoming friendly with someone from another culture; or a relative, friend, or stranger coming to live in your home.

2. What was the greatest change that you had to make when you went to a new school?

3. Have you ever read a book or seen a TV program about a place that you later visited? How different was the actual place?

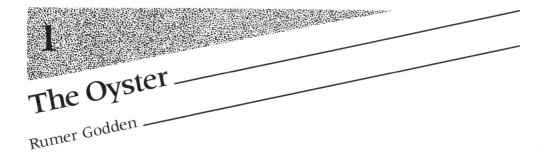

1

The Oyster

Rumer Godden

Rumer Godden was born in England in 1907, but she spent half of her life in India. She has written many stories and novels about life in India, and she writes very well about nature and human nature. Her popular works include the children's story *The Valiant Chatti-Maker* (1988) and the best seller *Black Narcissus. A House with Four Rooms*, an autobiography of her later years, was published in 1989.

The following selection is from her book *Mooltiki: Stories and Poems from India*. In the story from which this selection comes, "The Oyster," Gopal is an Indian student studying in London. On a trip to France he goes to a restaurant with a friend who orders raw (live) oysters. Gopal feels that he has to eat the oysters although he does not like them. Suddenly the shock of all his new experiences begins to affect him. In the selection below, he is writing home and trying to describe his feelings.

PRE-READING QUESTIONS

1. What are the most common kinds of food that are eaten at dinner in your home? At breakfast?

2. What foods are never eaten in your home? Why not?

3. What kinds of food do you *not* like? Why not?

4. Have you ever had to eat a food that you didn't like? If so, tell about that experience.

5. Some people eat only vegetables and grains. Why do you think they do this? Why do some people eat only certain kinds of meat?

Up to this evening, which should have been the most delightful of all, everything had been delightful. "Delightful" was Gopal's new word. "London is delightful," he wrote home. "The college is delightful, Professor William Morgan is delightful and so is Mrs. Morgan and the little Morgans, but perhaps," he added with pain, for he had to admit that the Morgan children were rough and spoiled, "perhaps not *as* delightful if you see them for a very long time. . . . The hostel is delightful. . . . I find my work delightful." He had planned to write home that Paris was delightful. "We went to a famous French restaurant in the rue Perpignan," he had meant to write, "it is called the Chez Perpignan. It is de—" Now tears made his dark eyes bright; he could not write that; it was not delightful at all.

Gopal's family lived in Bengal; they were Brahmini Hindus and his mother kept the household to orthodox ways in spite of all he and his elder brother could do. Now Gopal saw her orthodox food: the flat brass platters of rice, the pile of *luchis*—flaky, puffed, pale gold biscuits—the vegetable fritters fried crisp, the great bowl of lentil purée, and the small accompanying bowls of relishes—shredded coconut or fried onion or spinach or chilis in tomato sauce or chutney, all to be put on the rice. He saw fruit piled on banana leaves, the bowl of fresh curd, the milk or orange or bel-fruit juice in the silver drinking tumblers; no meat or fish, not even eggs, were eaten in that house. "We shall not take life," said his mother. Gopal looked down at his plate in the Perpignan and shuddered.

He had come to Europe with shining intentions, eager, anxious to do as the Romans did, as the English, the French, as Romans everywhere. "There will be things you will not be able to stomach," he had been warned; so far he had stomached everything. His elder brother Jai had been before him and had come back utterly accustomed to everything Western; when Jai and Tooni (Jai's wife) went out to dinner they had Western dishes; they ate meat, even beef, but not in their own home. "Not while I live," said his mother.

Glossary

up to until

rough difficult to control; undisciplined

hostel a building that offers students a room and meals at reasonable prices

orthodox generally accepted

crisp hard, dry

take life kill

shining intentions the best intentions

as the Romans did this refers to the saying, "When in Rome, do as the Romans do."

stomach accept, tolerate

Vocabulary

A. Find the word(s) closest in meaning to the underlined word(s). Circle the best answer.

1. We spent a <u>delightful</u> evening with them.
   a. funny   b. enjoyable   c. uninteresting   d. anxious

2. Gopal opened his mail <u>eagerly.</u>
   a. without enthusiasm   b. utterly
   c. with enthusiasm   d. carefully

3. We are <u>accustomed to</u> drinking milk at dinner.
   a. sick from   b. tired of   c. delighted by   d. used to

4. <u>In spite of</u> the weather, we began our journey.
   a. instead of   b. although   c. regardless of   d. for

5. I <u>shuddered</u> at the sight of the spinach.
   a. threw up   b. shook   c. moaned   d. wept

6. Their dog was very <u>spoiled.</u>
   a. sweet   b. well behaved   c. badly behaved   d. playful

B. Complete the sentences with words from the list.

accustomed to	delightful	bright	intention
in spite of	spoiled	orthodox	household
up to	rough	eager	shuddered

Gopal had been ___eager___ to go to Europe. His ___intention___ was to live like a Westerner. When Gopal wrote to his family, he wanted to tell them that everything in France was ___delightful___. And, ___up to___ that evening, everything had been delightful. But ___in spite of___ his eagerness to do as the French did, Gopal couldn't eat as the French did. There were still some foods that he was not ___accustomed to___. That evening in the French restaurant, Gopal looked down at his plate and ___shuddered___.

He thought of his mother, who was ___orthodox___ in her ways. She did not allow meat or fish in her ___household___. He thought of the Morgan children who were ___rough___ and ___spoiled___. Tears made his dark eyes ___bright___.

Comprehension

1. Why is Gopal writing to his parents?
2. How long had everything been delightful?
3. How do you know that Gopal was not a native of London?
4. Why was Gopal in London?
5. Did Gopal like London?
6. How did Gopal feel about the Morgan children? Did he like them as much as he liked Professor Morgan and his wife?
7. In writing to his family, what had Gopal planned to say about Paris?
8. Where did Gopal go "this evening" (line 1)?
9. Did Gopal and his older brother agree with their mother's orthodox ways?
10. Why didn't Gopal's mother eat meat or fish?
11. Where did Jai and Tooni eat meat?
12. What do you think happened that made Gopal cry?

Wordwork _____

CONNECTING IDEAS

A. Combine sentences into one sentence. You may have to change nouns to pronouns, and you may have to change the order of the sentences. Use the connectives such as *before*, *after*, or *when* to combine the sentences.

EXAMPLE

Tooni fell asleep. Tooni drank some wine.

Tooni fell asleep after she drank some wine.

1. He lived in Paris for two years. He went back home to India.

2. Gopal thought the Morgan family would be delightful. Gopal met the Morgan children.

3. Gopal had stomached everything. Gopal went to the Chez Perpignan restaurant.

4. Gopal went to Paris. He usually ate meals with no meat or fish.

5. Jai came back from Paris. He ate meat when he went out to dinner.

B. This is an exercise in combining three short sentences into one longer and better sentence. Each sentence will have two clauses connected with *but*. You may make other changes in the sentences.

EXAMPLE

The children were delightful. The children were rough. The children were spoiled.

The children were delightful, but they were rough, and spoiled.

1. Professor Morgan is delightful. Mrs. Morgan is delightful. The children are not as delightful.

   _____

   _____

2. They could eat vegetables at home. They could eat fruit at home. They couldn't eat meat at home.

   _____

   _____

3. Gopal wanted to try some Western ways. Gopal's brother wanted to try some Western ways. Gopal's mother wanted to keep to orthodox ways.

   _____

   _____

4. Gopal wanted to eat like the French. Gopal wanted to drink like the French. Gopal couldn't stomach the oysters.

   _____

   _____

Favorite Words

Often when we learn a new language we find a favorite word, and we use it a lot. Gopal, for example, has discovered the word _delightful._

1. What are three English words that you like to use a lot?

   _____   _____   _____

2. Sometimes words in a foreign language sound funny to us. Are there any English words that sound funny to you?

Compare your words to those of other students.

To Travel is to Broaden the Mind

A. Living in a new place affects people differently. Some things which affect the experience of a person in a new place are the place itself, the age of the person, the purpose of the trip, and the length of time away from home.

1. How old do you think Gopal is?

2. How does travel affect old people? young people? children?

3. When people are away on a trip for a long time, what kinds of things make them unhappy?

4. When people are away for a long time, what kinds of things do they miss?

5. Have you ever left your country to study or travel? Was it a delightful experience?

B. List some things that you find/found delightful about a new place. Also list some things that are/were not delightful.

Delightful	Not delightful
EXAMPLE	
eating new foods	losing my luggage

C. Tell why you didn't like some of the "not delightful" things.

D. "There will be some things that you will not be able to *stomach.*" What are some other words that you can substitute for the word *stomach*?

Homesick

Homesick is an adjective that describes how people feel when they are away from home and they miss their home very much.

1. What are some things that you miss when you are away from home?

   _____   _____

   _____   _____

   _____   _____

   _____   _____

2. Complete the following sentences.

   a. I feel homesick whenever _____.

   b. Sometimes I feel homesick when _____.

3. Write two sentences that describe some things that you can't do any-more because you are not at home. Use the word *anymore*.

   EXAMPLE

   _____ *I can't run with my dog anymore.* _____

   a. _____

   b. _____

4. What is one thing that you do to make yourself feel better when you are homesick?

   _____

   Compare your answer to those of other students.

5. What do you think family or friends could do to make people feel less homesick?

   _____

   Compare your answer to those of other students.

6. Many American children who go to overnight camp for the first time feel homesick at first. Camp directors tell parents not to worry. They tell parents not to write letters that say "We miss you so much" or "The house is empty without you." Do you think this is good advice? What other advice would you give to parents of campers?

   _____

   _____

Writing Letters

1. What do you write about when you write letters to your family and friends?

   _____

   _____

2. What kinds of things do your relatives write about in their letters to you? What kinds of questions do your friends and relatives ask you?

   _____

   _____

A House Is Not a Home

1. What is the difference between a house and a home?

   _____

   _____

2. How is the word *home* translated in your language? Does it mean the same thing as *home* in English?

   _____

   _____

Old Ways and New Ways

1. What was Gopal's mother's attitude toward the customs of her daily life? How do you know what her attitude was?

2. How did Gopal and his brother Jai feel about their mother's attitude?

3. How has Gopal reacted to the new customs he found in England and France?

4. Tell or write about a new custom that you became accustomed to when you lived in a place different from your home.

5. Tell or write about a new custom that you couldn't become accustomed to when you lived in a place different from your home.

Suggestions for Discussion and Writing _____

1. Imagine that you are visiting your favorite city away from home. Write a letter to your family describing your experiences in the city.

2. Imagine that you are visiting a city that you do not like. Write a letter to your family describing your unpleasant experiences.

3. What are some of the difficulties one encounters in a restaurant in an unfamiliar city? Describe an experience that you or a friend may have had.

4. Describe an experience that should have been better than it was.

5. Describe an experience that was better than you expected it to be.

6. Imagine that you have received a letter from a relative who is "doing as the Romans do" in his travels. Write such a letter.

7. What do you think happened after Gopal shuddered? What do you think that his friend said? Imagine the conversation between them. Do you think that Gopal told his friend the truth about his feelings?

Independent Study _____

1. Read another short story by Rumer Godden or read the rest of "The Oyster" in *Mooltiki: Stories and Poems from India*.

2. Read parts of the novel *Homesick—My Own Story* by Jean Fritz. This is a story about a young girl coming to the United States and observing its customs.

3. Read *Arthur Goes to Camp* by Marc Brown. This is an amusing children's story in which Arthur goes away to camp for the first time.

4. Interview someone who has gone to overnight camp. Ask them if they felt homesick. Did they try to call their parents? Did they try to run away?

5. Describe an instance when you were served a food that you did not like at all. Did you try to eat it?

The Oyster **11**

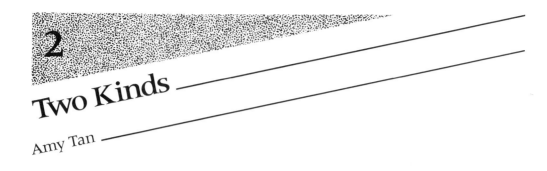

2

Two Kinds

Amy Tan

Amy Tan is a writer who lives in California, where she was born in 1952. Her parents had moved to the United States a few years earlier, and Tan grew up speaking English and Chinese.

The following selection is from her first book *The Joy Luck Club*, which focuses on the hopes and dreams of four mothers and their daughters. In this selection, Jing-Mei (Tan) talks about her mother's plans for her to become a prodigy.

PRE-READING QUESTIONS

1. When you were a child, did you have any dreams of becoming famous? What did you dream of? Where did you get the idea?

2. Did your mother or father ever tell people that you were very smart or very beautiful or very talented? How did you feel when they did that?

3. Can you remember when you first disobeyed your parents?

4. When do you think that you first showed your independence from your parents?

5. Do your parents (or relatives) agree with your (future) career plans?

My mother believed you could be anything you wanted to be in America. You could open a restaurant. You could work for the government and get good retirement. You could buy a house with almost no money down. You could become rich. You could become instantly famous.

"Of course you can be prodigy, too," my mother told me when I was nine. "You can be best anything. What does Auntie Lindo know? Her daughter, she is only best tricky." *Smart*

America was where all my mother's hopes lay. She had come here in 1949 after losing everything in China: her mother and father, her family home, her first husband, and two daughters, twin baby girls. But she never looked back with regret. There were so many ways for things to get better.

Every night after dinner, my mother and I would sit at the Formica kitchen table. She would present new tests, taking her examples from stories of amazing children she had read in *Ripley's Believe It or Not*, or *Good Housekeeping, Reader's Digest*, and a dozen other magazines she kept in a pile in our bathroom. My mother got these magazines from people whose houses she cleaned. And since she cleaned many houses each week, we had a great assortment. She would look through them all, searching for stories about remarkable children.

The first night she brought out a story about a three-year-old boy who knew the capitals of all the states and even most of the European countries. A teacher was quoted as saying the little boy could also pronounce the names of the foreign cities correctly.

"What's the capital of Finland?" my mother asked me, looking at the magazine story.

All I knew was the capital of California, because Sacramento was the name of the street we lived on in Chinatown. "Nairobi!" I guessed, saying the most foreign word I could think of. She checked to see if that was possibly one way to pronounce "Helsinki" before showing me the answer.

The tests got harder—multiplying numbers in my head, finding the queen of hearts in a deck of cards, trying to stand on my head without using my hands, predicting the daily temperatures in Los Angeles, New York, and London.

One night I had to look at a page from the Bible for three minutes and then report everything I could remember. "Now Jehoshaphat had riches and honor in abundance and . . . that's all I remember, Ma," I said.

And after seeing my mother's disappointed face once again, something inside of me began to die. I hated the tests, the raised hopes and failed expectations. Before going to bed that night, I looked in the mirror above the bathroom sink and when I saw only my face staring back—and that it would always be this ordinary face—I began to cry. Such a sad, ugly girl! I made highpitched noises like a crazed animal, trying to scratch out the face in the mirror.

And then I saw what seemed to be the prodigy side of me—because I had never seen that face before. I looked at my reflection, blinking so I could see more clearly. The girl staring back at me was angry, powerful. This girl and I were the same. I had new thoughts, willful thoughts, or rather thoughts filled with lots of won'ts. I won't let her change me, I promised myself. I won't be what I'm not.

Glossary

money down   paying only part of the cost at the time you buy something
Chinatown   a section of San Francisco where many Chinese people live
deck of cards   a pack of playing cards

Vocabulary

A. Find the word(s) closest in meaning to the underlined word(s). Circle the best answer.

1. A <u>famous</u> person is someone who is _____.
   a. smart   b. large   c. secret   d. well-known

2. A <u>prodigy</u> is someone who has _____.
   a. unusual ability   b. a great deal of pride
   c. very little ability   d. reached old age

3. A feeling of <u>regret</u> is a feeling of _____ that something has or has not been done.
   a. happiness   b. anger   c. sadness   d. jealousy

4. The book had stories about <u>remarkable</u> children.
   a. angry   b. blinded   c. powerful   d. extraordinary

B. Complete the sentences with words from the list. A few words must be used more than once.

regret	disappointed	correctly	guessed
prodigy	remarkable	change	promised
tests	ordinary	checked	

Jing-Mei's mother was not an ⟨₁⟩ _____ woman. She had lost everything in China, but she did not look back in ⟨₂⟩ _____. In California, she decided that her daughter could become anything she wanted to. She wanted her to become a ⟨₃⟩ _____, so she gave her ⟨₄⟩ _____ to improve her knowledge. Jing-Mei ⟨₅⟩ _____ at the answers to the tests, and her mother ⟨₆⟩ _____ her to see if she had answered the questions ⟨₇⟩ _____. But Jing-Mei's mother was ⟨₈⟩ _____ when she saw that her daughter did not have a ⟨₉⟩ _____ memory. Jing-Mei knew that she was not a ⟨₁₀⟩ _____; she was just an ⟨₁₁⟩ _____ girl, and she ⟨₁₂⟩ _____ herself that she wouldn't let her mother ⟨₁₃⟩ _____ her.

Comprehension

1. What happened to Jing-Mei's mother in China?
2. What did Jing-Mei's mother believe about America?
3. What did Jing-Mei's mother expect of her daughter?
4. Why did Jing-Mei's mother ask her about the capital of Finland?
5. Why was Jing-Mei's mother disappointed?
6. What did Jing-Mei think when she looked in the mirror?
7. What was the "prodigy side" of Jing-Mei?

Wordwork

CONNECTING IDEAS

A. Combine the sentences into one sentence. Sometimes you may have to change nouns into pronouns. Use the connective *that* to combine the sentences.

EXAMPLE

My mother believed something. You could be anything you want in America.

My mother believed that you could be anything you want in America.

1. My mother believed something. You could open a restaurant in America.

2. My mother believed something. You could buy a house with almost no money down.

3. My mother believed something. I could be a prodigy.

4. She thought something. She was a sad, ugly girl.

5. He thought something. He wouldn't be able to change.

B. Combine these sentences using *who* or *that*.

EXAMPLE

She read a story about a boy. The boy knew all the capitals of the United States.

She read a story about a boy who knew all the capitals of the United States.

1. Her mother was interested in children. The children were prodigies.

2. Her mother read stories about children. The stories were in popular magazines.

3. My father got a lot of magazines. The magazines were in the houses he cleaned.

4. Sacramento was the name of a street. The street was in Chinatown.

_____

5. In the mirror there was a girl. The girl was angry and powerful.

_____

I Thought I Could

Jing-Mei's mother thought that Jing-Mei could become instantly famous in America. Complete the sentences below describing what you or someone you know thought they could do.

1. I thought that I could _____.

2. My uncle thought that he could _____.

3. My best friend thought that _____.

4. My sister thought that _____.

Regrets

Do you think that Jing-Mei regretted that she was not a prodigy? Complete the following sentences with things that you regret. You can regret something that you did or did not do. Or you can regret something that someone else did or did not do.

1. I regret that I _____.

2. I regret that _____.

3. I regret that _____.

Tests

1. Find out if there is a memory prodigy in your class. The instructor or a student can bring in a page of information. Everyone will read it for 30 seconds. Then everyone will write down what they remember. The one with the most information will be the Memory Prodigy.

2. Do this exercise in pairs. Write down the names of ten countries and ask a classmate to write down the capitals of those countries. Exchange lists.

3. Are there any English names of cities, states, rivers, etc. that you have trouble pronouncing? Make a list and compare it with those of other students.

4. Children often test each other, physically and mentally. What are some tests that you and your friends used when you were children?

Hopes and Expectations

Complete the sentences below by indicating three hopes or expectations. Then write two sentences of your own.

1. I hope that _____.

2. My parents hope that _____.

3. We should all hope that _____.

4. _____.

5. _____.

The Face

Describe the face of someone you know. You can use some of these words and you can add your own.

hair	beard	brown	sad
eyes	mustache	black	happy
eyebrows	chin	blue	light
eyelashes	lips	green	dark
cheeks	mouth	gray	smooth
skin	teeth	blond	rough
		brunette	soft
			hard

Wills and Won'ts

Jing-Mei had thoughts filled with wills and won'ts. List some things that you intend to do or not intend to do.

I will _____. I won't _____.

I will _____. I won't _____.

Suggestions for Discussion and Writing

1. Jing-Mei says, "I won't be what I'm not." Many people try to be what they are not. Describe someone you know like that.

2. Jing-Mei realizes something about herself when she looks in the mirror. Can you remember a moment when you realized something about yourself? If so, describe it.

3. Jing-Mei's mother is living in a new culture and she has ideas about it that may not be accurate. Describe some ideas you had about a place you visited or went to live in that were not accurate. Write two paragraphs, one describing your ideas before you went and one describing your ideas after you went.

   Before I went to _____, I thought _____

   _____

   _____

   _____

   _____

   After I went to _____, I thought _____

   _____

   _____

   _____

   _____

Independent Study

1. Read *The Joy Luck Club* by Amy Tan.

2. Wolfgang Amadeus Mozart has been referred to as "The Wonder Boy." Read about his early life and why people thought he was a prodigy.

3. Go to the library and find an article about conflicts between parents and children.

4. Go to the library and do some research about child prodigies. Write a few paragraphs about your findings.

3

Lucy
Jamaica Kincaid

This is from a story about a young woman named Lucy. After living on an island in the Caribbean for the first 19 years of her life, Lucy decides to leave her family and her country. She gets a job as an "au pair," working for a wealthy family. The couple, Lewis and Mariah, have three children and live in an apartment in a large city in the United States. At the time of the story below, Lucy has been working for the couple for almost a year and has now decided to leave the job and find her own place to live. At the same time, the marriage of Lewis and Mariah is falling apart, and life in the apartment is rather sad.

The story centers on Lucy's feelings about herself and others as she develops her personality. She is not sure exactly who she is, but she knows that she is no longer the girl who lived on that island.

PRE-READING QUESTIONS

1. In what ways have you changed during the last five or ten years?

2. Are there any differences between what your family expects of you and what you expect of yourself?

3. Have you ever felt that you wanted to leave your family to live by yourself or with friends? What made you feel that way? What did you expect the advantages to be?

4. To what extent does the weather affect your feelings?

It was January again; the world was thin and pale and cold again; I was making a new beginning again.

I had been a girl of whom certain things were expected, none of them too bad: a career as a nurse, for example; a sense of duty to my parents; obedience to the law and worship of convention. But in one year of being away from home, that girl had gone out of existence.

The person I had become I did not know very well. Oh, on the outside everything was familiar. My hair was the same, though now I wore it cut close to my head, and this made my face seem almost perfectly round, and so for the first time ever I entertained the idea that I might actually be beautiful. I knew that if I ever decided I was beautiful I would not make too big a thing of it. My eyes were the same. My ears were the same. The other important things about me were the same.

But the things I could not see about myself, the things I could not put my hands on—those things had changed, and I did not yet know them well. I understood that I was inventing myself, and that I was doing this more in the way of a painter than in the way of a scientist. I could not count on precision or calculation; I could only count on intuition. I did not have anything exactly in mind, but when the picture was complete I would know. I did not have position, I did not have money at my disposal. I had memory, I had anger, I had despair.

I was born on an island, a very small island, twelve miles long and eight miles wide; yet when I left it at nineteen years of age I had never set foot on three-quarters of it. I had recently met someone who was born on the other side of the world from me but had visited this island on which my family had lived for generations; this person, a woman, said to me, "What a beautiful place," and she named a village by the sea and then went on to describe a view that was unknown to me. At the time I was so ashamed I could hardly make a reply, for I had come to believe that people in my position in the world should know everything about the place they are from.

When I told Mariah that I was leaving, she said, "It's not a year yet. You are supposed to stay for at least a year." Her voice was full of anger, but I ignored it. It's always hard for the person who is left behind. And even as she said it she must have known how hollow it sounded, for it was only a matter of weeks before it would be a year since I had come to live with her. The reality of her situation was now clear to her: she was a woman whose husband had betrayed her. I wanted to say this to her: "Your situation is an everyday thing. Men behave in this way all the time. The ones who do not behave in this way are the exceptions to the rule." But I knew what her response would have been. She would have said, "What a cliché." She would have said, "What do you know about these things?" And she would have been right; it was a cliché, and I had no personal experience of a thing like that. But all the same, where I came from every woman knew this cliché, and a man like Lewis would not have been a surprise; his behavior would not have cast a pall over any woman's life. It was expected. Everybody knew that men have no morals, that they do not know how to behave, that they do not know how to treat other people. It was why men like laws so much; it was why they had to invent such things— they need a guide. When they are not sure what to do, they consult this guide. If the guide gives them advice they don't like, they change the guide. This was something I knew; why didn't Mariah know it, also? And if I were to tell it to her she would only show me a book she had somewhere which contradicted everything I said—a book most likely written by a woman who understood absolutely nothing.

The holidays came, and they did feel like a funeral, for so many things had died. For the children's sake, she and Lewis put up a good front. He came and went, doing all the things he would have done if he were still living with them. He bought the fir tree, bought the children the presents they wanted, bought Mariah a coat made up from the skins of small pesty animals who lived in the ground. She, of course, hated it, but for appearances' sake kept her opinion to herself. He must have forgotten that she was not the sort of person who would wear the skin of another being if she could help it. Or perhaps in the rush of things he gave his old love his new love's present. Mariah gave me a necklace made up of pretty porcelain beads and small polished balls of wood. She said it was the handiwork of someone in Africa. It was the most beautiful thing anyone had ever given me.

The New Year came, and I was going somewhere new again. I gathered my things together; I had a lot more than when I first came. I had new clothes, all better suited to this new climate I now lived in. I had a camera and prints of the photographs I had taken, prints I had made myself. But mostly I had books—so many books, and they were mine; I would not have to part with them. It had always been a dream of mine to just own a lot of books, to never part with a book once I had read it. So there they were, resting nicely in small boxes—my own books, the books that I had read. Mariah spoke to me harshly all the time now, and she began to make up rules which she insisted that I follow; and I did, for after all what else could she do? It was a last resort for her—insisting that I be the servant and she the master. She used to insist that we be friends, but that had apparently not worked out very well, for now I was leaving. The master business did not become her at all, and it made me sad to see her that way. Still, it made me remember what my mother had said to me many times: for my whole life I should make sure the roof over my head was my own; such a thing was important, especially if you were a woman.

On the day I actually left, there was no sun; the sky had shut it out tightly. It was a Saturday. Lewis had taken the children to eat snails at a French restaurant. All four of them liked such things— and just as well, for that went with the life they were expected to lead eventually. Mariah helped me put my things in a taxi. It was a cold goodbye on her part. Her voice and her face were stony. She did not hug me. I did not take any of this personally; someday we would be friends again. I was numb, but it was from not knowing just what this new life would hold for me.

Glossary

put (my) hands on   understand easily

count on   depend on

cliché   an idea or expression that has been used too much

cast a pall   produce a dark covering; create sadness

put up a good front   face a situation with pretended confidence

a last resort   a last possibility

did not become her   was not appropriate for her

Vocabulary

A. Find the word(s) closest in meaning to the underlined word(s). Circle the best answer.

1. The house looked so <u>familiar</u> that I kept thinking about it all evening.
   a. famous   b. known   c. unknown   d. harsh

2. She had a look of <u>despair</u> about her.
   a. without hope   b. without strength
   c. without pride   d. without sadness

3. Everyone could see that he was <u>guilty</u>.
   a. sad   b. pale   c. wrong   d. free

4. My mother looked at me with <u>annoyance</u>.
   a. irritation   b. pride   c. excitement   d. sadness

5. I was <u>supposed to</u> become a professional dancer.
   a. ready to   b. trying to   c. expected to   d. hoping to

B. Complete the sentences with words from the list. There may be more than one good choice for each blank.

expected	familiar	despair
behaved	numb	exception
supposed to	beautiful	opinion
ignored	cold	
contradicted		

Lucy was _____ stay with Mariah and Lewis for a year, but the atmosphere of the apartment had become _____. Lewis had found another woman. Now when Mariah spoke, her voice was full of _____. Yet Lewis _____ the problem and _____ as if he were still living in a _____ family. In Lucy's _____, Lewis' behavior was not an _____ to the rule. Men like Lewis were _____ to her. She wanted to explain that to Mariah, but she was afraid that Mariah might find a book which _____ Lucy's ideas on men. When Lucy finally left the apartment, she felt _____ because she didn't know

what she _____ from the new life ahead of her.

Comprehension _____

1. What time of year is it?
2. What did Lucy's parents expect of her?
3. What did Lucy imagine when she thought about her physical appearance?
4. Why was Lucy ashamed when she met someone who had visited her island?
5. What was Mariah's problem?
6. What were Lucy's ideas about the behavior of men? Was she surprised at Lewis' behavior?
7. How did Mariah and Lewis "put up a good front" during the holidays?
8. What advice from her mother did Lucy remember?

Wordwork _____
CONNECTING IDEAS

Combine the sentences into one sentence. Sometimes you may have to change nouns into pronouns. Use *because* or *since* to connect the sentences.

EXAMPLE

Lucy decided to live with them. Lucy needed a job and a place to stay.

_____*Lucy decided to live with them because*_____
_____*she needed a job and a place to stay.*_____

1. Lucy's face seemed round. Lucy had her hair cut close to her head.

_____

_____

2. Lucy felt ashamed. Lucy met someone who knew more about the island than she did.

_____

_____

3. Mariah became angry when Lucy left. Lucy was supposed to work for Mariah for a year.

_____

_____

4. Lucy was not surprised at Lewis' behavior. Lucy thought that Lewis did not know how to behave.

_____

_____

5. Lewis brought gifts for the children. It was Christmastime.

_____

_____

Duties and Obligations

1. Lucy's parents expected her to do certain things. They thought that she had duties and obligations. List some things that your parents, teachers, or friends expect you to do.

   EXAMPLE

   _____ *My parents expect me to clean my room.* _____

   a. _____

   b. _____

   c. _____

2. There are things that we feel that we should do (such as study another language) and there are things that we have to do (such as pay our taxes).

   What are some things you feel that you should do?

   a. I feel that I should _____.

   b. _____

   c. _____

   Compare your answers with those of your classmates.

What are some things that you have to do?

a. I have to _____

b. _____

c. _____

Compare your answers with those of your classmates.

3. Laws, which are obligations that we have to the community we live in, are different in different communities. Describe one difference in laws between two communities that you are familiar with.

_____

_____

_____

_____

Follow the Rules

Mariah insisted that Lucy follow certain rules. Complete the following sentences. Notice the form of the verb that follows *insist*.

EXAMPLE

My mother insists _____ *that my brother wash his own laundry.* _____

1. My teacher insisted that I _____

2. My roommate insists that we _____

3. The doctor insisted that the patient _____

4. The children insisted that their mother _____

5. The car salesperson insists that _____

6. Our neighbors insist that _____

From Home

Lucy realizes that she has changed since she left her island. "In one year away from home that girl had gone out of existence."

1. If you have left home, what change(s) have you noticed in yourself?

   _____

   _____

2. What changes have you noticed in a friend or relative who has lived away from home for some time?

   _____

   _____

The Days Went By

Lucy says that the days went by too slowly and too quickly.

1. Describe a time in your life when you felt that the days went by too slowly.

   _____

   _____

2. Describe a time in your life when the days went by too quickly.

   _____

   _____

3. Was there a time in your life when the days went by too slowly and too quickly? Describe it.

   _____

   _____

Your Own Roof

1. Lucy's mother told her that she should make sure that the roof over her head was her own. What does this mean?

   _____

   _____

   _____

2. What are some ways that young adults today can make sure that the roof over their heads is their own?

   _____

   _____

   _____

Suggestions for Discussion and Writing _____

1. Write a paragraph about how you will make sure that you have a roof of your own over your head.

2. Write one or two paragraphs about a beautiful place that you know very well. Describe what it looks like and who goes there. If the place is interesting historically or culturally, add that information as well.

3. Lucy says that men who do not behave like Lewis are "exceptions to the rule." What is the rule? What are some other "rules" about behavior of men and women? Are these rules the same from one culture to another?

4. What kind of coat do you think that Lewis gave Mariah?

5. What do you think is going to happen to Lucy after she leaves Mariah's apartment? Where do you think she is going to live?

Independent Study

1. Find a description of a woman who is supposed to be beautiful. Choose some words from that description and describe someone that you know.

2. Find a description of a man who is supposed to be handsome. What are some of the words used to describe him? Describe someone that you know using some of those adjectives.

3. Find a description of a child. What are some of the words used to describe the child?

4. Take a photograph or draw a picture of your ideal "home away from home." Then describe the most important characteristics.

5. Read the entire story of *Lucy*. Or read another story by Jamaica Kincaid and be prepared to tell or write about it.

Review

Wednesday Jan. 5. *choose 3 or 4.*

1. Do you think Gopal will remain in France? Do you think Jing-Mei and Lucy will remain in the United States? Tell why or why not.

2. In each of the stories in this unit, a character imagines something. Who are these characters and what do they imagine?

3. If you wanted to live in another country and you had to work there, which country would you choose and what kind of work would you do?

4. If you could study in any country that you wanted, which country would you choose and what would you study?

5. Imagine that Gopal, Jing-Mei, and Lucy were at the same school. Would all three be friends with each other? If they went out to dinner together, where would they go?

6. In his book *That Fine Italian Hand*, Paul Hofman writes that we can realize the values of a people when we observe their daily life. He describes coffee bars in Italy—very clean, sparkling, with chromium, bright marble, clear colors, and neon lights. He says that coffee bars represent what Italians really like: a happy place that looks modern, with a lot of light, a place where people can talk in loud voices for a short time, and a place where the service is quick. They don't like places that also serve food because the smell of the food spoils the good smell of the coffee. Hofman then considers the differences between an Italian coffee bar, an English pub, a German beer-hall, and a French café.

   Describe a similar place in your country where you like to go and tell why you like it.

7. In "How to Get Ready for Studying Abroad," Roger Cox says you must "stay loose." What does he mean? Do you think Gopal, Jing-Mei, and Lucy stay loose? Which one is the loosest?

UNIT TWO
Relationships

UNIT INTRODUCTION

The stories in this unit focus on family relationships. In "Mother Dear and Daddy," Junius Edwards describes a family that is broken up by an accident that has killed the mother and father. In "Significant Moments in the Life of My Mother," the main character of the story looks back and remembers the stories her mother used to tell and the important part they played in her family life. Harry Petrakis, in "The Last Escapade," puts us into the middle of a family conflict. The father in the story has some ideas about how he wants to live his life, and those ideas surprise his son and daughter.

UNIT PRE-READING

1. Do you think differently about your family life now than when you were younger? What are some differences?

2. What are some of the pleasures of growing up in a family? What are some of the problems?

3. What are some of the major sources of conflict between parents and children?

4. What are the advantages of being an only child? What are the advantages of having several brothers and sisters?

Mother Dear and Daddy

Junius Edwards

Junius Edwards (b. 1929) grew up in Louisiana and studied in Chicago and Oslo, Norway. He is the author of three well-known short stories as well as the novel *If We Must Die*, which was first published in 1961.

The story "Mother Dear and Daddy" is included in several collections of short stories by African-American writers. In the story, five children living in the southern part of the United States learn that their mother and father have been killed in an automobile accident. In the selection below, we read about the reaction of twelve-year old Jim, the oldest child.

PRE-READING QUESTIONS

1. Was there a time when something happened that changed the life of your family significantly? Describe it.

2. Do you remember hearing bad news when you were younger? How did you or your family react to it?

3. Do you know any children who had to move to a new home because of a death or a divorce? How did they adjust to the new home?

4. Did anything ever happen to you that you couldn't believe would happen? Describe it.

"What we going to do, Aunt Mabel?"

"Lord knows, son. Lord knows," Aunt Mabel said, sitting in her rocker, moving, slow, back and forth, looking down at me, on my knees, my arms resting on her huge right thigh and my head turned up to her, watching that round face, her lips tight now, her head shaking side to side, and her eyes clouded, and me not understanding her answer.

"The Lord giveth and the Lord taketh away."

But, what we going to do? I could not understand Aunt Mabel. I did not know what her mumbling about The Lord had to do with this. All I knew was she had just told me Mother Dear and Daddy were dead. Mother Dear and Daddy were dead. Mother Dear and Daddy would not come back. Mother Dear and Daddy wouldn't take us home again. What we going to do?

"I want to go home. I want to go home," I screamed and got to my feet and ran to the door, realizing it was Aunt Mabel calling my name. I ran out to the yard where John and our sisters played, and right past them. I was at our house, running up the steps across the porch, as fast as I could, straight to the screened door, wham! and I lay on my back on the porch looking up at the screen, at the imprints made in it by my head and hands and my right knee. I got right up and started banging on the door, trying to twist the knob.

"Mother Dear! Daddy! Mother Dear! Daddy!" I called as loud as I could and kept banging on the door. Then, I ran to the back door and called again and banged and kicked the door. They did not come.

They would not come.

"Mother Dear! Daddy! It's me. Let me in. Open the door!"

They would not come.

I ran to the front, out to the street and turned and looked up to their room and saw the shades were drawn just as they were drawn when Mother Dear and Daddy took us over to Aunt Mabel's house to stay for the weekend while they went away fishing with cousin Bob.

I cupped my hands up to my mouth.

"Mother Dear. Daddy. Mother Dear! Daddy!"

I called, and called again and all the while I kept my eyes glued on that window, waiting. Any moment now, any second now, now, *now*, waited to see that white shade zoom up and then the window, and then Mother Dear and Daddy, both together, lean out, smiling, laughing, waving, calling my name, now, now, *now*.

They did not come.

They would not come. The shade stood still, stayed still, with the sun shining on it through the window pane; stayed still, as if the sun were a huge nail shooting through the pane and holding it down. It did not go up. It would not go up.

They would not come.

I knew it. Suddenly, just like that, snap, I knew they would not come; could not come. The shades would stay still. I knew they would not come. I lowered my hands, my eyes darting from shaded window to shaded window, around the yard, under the house, searching, for what? I did not know, and then there was the car. My eyes were glued to the car, and I started over to it, slowly at first, and then I ran and I stopped short and pressed my head up against the glass in the front door beside the steering wheel. The glass was hot on my nose and lips and forehead, and burned them, but I did not care, I pressed harder, as if by doing so I could push right through the glass, not breaking it, but melting through it. Then, I felt as though I *was* inside, in my favorite spot up front with Daddy, and in back were Mother Dear and John and our sisters; Daddy whistling and the trees going by and the farms and green, green, green, and other cars and Daddy starting to sing and all of us joining him singing "Choo-choo Train to Town," even Jo Ann and Willie Mae, who had not learned the words yet, singing, singing, and ending laughing and feeling Daddy's hand on my head.

"Jim," I turned from the window, and it was Aunt Mabel's hand on my head.

"Come on, son." She took my right hand and led me up the street as if I were a baby just starting to walk.

Glossary

What we going to do? What are we going to do? In some informal African-American speech, the verb *to be* is left out. There are several instances of this omission in this selection.

Lord knows only God knows

The Lord giveth and the Lord taketh away *giveth* and *taketh* are old forms of *gives* and *takes*. This kind of language may be found in the Bible.

got to my feet stood up

drawn down

stopped short stopped suddenly

Vocabulary

A. Find the word(s) closest in meaning to the underlined word. Circle the best answer.

1. Aunt Mabel was <u>mumbling</u> in a very low voice.
   - a. speaking unclearly
   - b. speaking clearly
   - c. crying
   - d. moaning

2. Jim ran <u>past</u> his brother John.
   - a. up to
   - b. farther than
   - c. together with
   - d. faster than

3. The shade didn't go up or down; it stood <u>still.</u>
   - a. moving slowly
   - b. at the top
   - c. without moving
   - d. at the bottom

4. His eyes <u>darted</u> from the car to the house to the yard.
   - a. moved slowly
   - b. didn't move
   - c. moved quickly
   - d. moved like glue

5. Jim was <u>searching</u> for his mother and father.
   - a. looking
   - b. crying
   - c. asking
   - d. waiting

B. Complete the sentences with words from the list.

kicked   across   to
twisted   on   up
screamed   past   around
banged   through   into

Jim knew there was trouble. He _____ in a loud voice, "I want to go home," and he started running. He ran _____ his sisters and _____ the yard. Then he darted _____ the stairs and ran _____ the screened door. He _____ on the door and _____ the knob. When nobody answered, he _____ the door. He wanted to go _____ the door and get inside, but he couldn't. He looked _____ the yard for some sign of his mother and father, but he didn't see them. Finally, Aunt Mabel put her hand _____ his head and led him _____ the street.

Comprehension

1. What did Aunt Mabel tell Jim when he asked her what they were going to do?
2. How did Jim find out that his parents were dead?
3. What happened when he ran to the screened door?
4. Why were the shades drawn?
5. When did Jim realize that his parents were not coming back?
6. What did he think about when he went to the car?
7. What is the meaning of the last sentence of the selection?

Wordwork

CONNECTING IDEAS

Combine the sentences into one sentence using the word *while*. You may have to change some nouns in the second sentence to pronouns. Study the example.

EXAMPLE

They came in the night. We were sleeping.

They came in the night while we were sleeping.

1. I giggled. My sisters sang.

   I giggled while my sisters sang.

2. We stayed with Aunt Mabel. Our parents went away fishing.

   We stayed with Aunt Mabel while our parents went away fishing.

3. Aunt Mabel put her hand on my head. Aunt Mabel talked to me softly.

   Aunt Mabel put her hand on my head while she talked to me softly.

4. I screamed their names. I twisted the doorknob.

   I screamed their name while I twisted the doorknob.

5. I kicked the door. My brothers were watching me.

   I kicked the door while my brothers were watching me.

6. My Daddy used to whistle. My Daddy was driving the car.

   My Daddy used to whistle while he was driving the car.

7. The boys used to sing. The boys were riding to town.

   The boys used to sing while they were riding to town.

What Are They Going to Do?

The children's parents have died. Use the phrase *going to* and describe some of the things you think the children and relatives are going to do.

EXAMPLE

The children are going to leave their home.

Mother Dear and Daddy **39**

1. _____
2. _____
3. _____
4. _____
5. _____

Family Names

Members of a family have names. For example, the father of a father is called a grandfather and the son of a grandfather's son is a grandson.

1. Write the names of family members that you found in this selection.

   _____

   _____

2. Write some other family names that you know.

   _____

   _____

3. Is "Mother Dear" a common expression for mothers? If not, what are some common English words for mothers?

   _____

   _____

4. What are some common English words for father?

   _____

   _____

5. Do you have a nickname or special name that family members call you?

   _____

My Favorite Spot

One of Jim's favorite spots was in his father's car. Write a paragraph describing one of your favorite spots and tell why it is a favorite spot.

40 *Relationships*

Wham!

This selection has some words that are used in English to describe certain kinds of sounds. Some of those words and some other words like them are listed below. What kinds of actions do you think these words describe?

EXAMPLE

plop _____ *the sound of pudding falling on the floor* _____

1. wham _____

2. zoom _____

3. chug _____

4. snap _____

5. puff _____

6. ah-choo _____

7. _____ _____

8. _____ _____

Suggestions for Discussion and Writing _____

1. What does Jim remember about his family life? What kind of a family do you think it was?

2. What is Aunt Mabel's attitude toward the death of the parents? How is it different from Jim's attitude?

3. This selection describes the loss of parents. Describe some of the reactions and effects when you or a family member had a loss.

4. Do you know any children who grew up without a mother or father? Describe the events that caused it.

5. Why did the writer have Jim tell the story (instead of Aunt Mabel, for example)?

Independent Study

1. Read Chapter 16 of the book *Death in the Family* by James Agee and compare the reactions of the boy in that story with Jim's reactions.

2. Retell the story with Aunt Mabel as the narrator. Imagine that she is telling the story about Jim.

3. Look up these words and be prepared to describe the differences in meaning: *snap, crack, slap, clap, tap, rap, knock.*

4. Look up these words and be prepared to describe the differences in meaning: *dart, dash, hurtle, gallop, scurry.*

5. Jim repeated the words "Mother Dear and Daddy." He was hoping that, by saying those words, he could get his parents to come back. Many people believe that words can have a special power. Give an example of a word or expression that is believed to have a special power among a particular group of people.

6. Find out what a family tree is. Draw a brief family tree for your own family.

7. Describe the ideas in this anonymous Eskimo poem.

"Magic Words"

In the very earliest time,
when both people and animals lived on earth,
a person could become an animal if he wanted to
and an animal could become a human being.
Sometimes they were people
and sometimes animals
and there was no difference.
All spoke the same language.
That was the time when words were like magic.
The human mind had mysterious powers.
A word spoken by chance
might have strange consequences.
It would suddenly come alive
and what people wanted to happen could happen—
all you had to do was say it.
Nobody could explain this:
That's the way it was.

8. There are many expressions to describe someone who is moving quickly. For example, we may say "She runs like lightning." Ask other people what they say to describe someone who moves quickly. Write four different expressions. Write four expressions to describe someone who moves slowly.

a. Someone who moves quickly

_____

_____

_____

_____

b. Someone who moves slowly

_____

_____

_____

_____

2

Significant Moments in the Life of My Mother

Margaret Atwood

Margaret Atwood (b. 1939) is a well-known Canadian writer. She has published nine novels, twenty collections of poetry, and numerous other works of fiction and nonfiction. She has won many literary awards, and her novel *The Handmaid's Tale* was on the best-seller list for several months. One of Atwood's short story collections is *Bluebeard's Egg*, from which the following selection is taken.

PRE-READING QUESTIONS

1. Do you believe that men and women behave differently? In what ways? In what situations?

2. In what ways are you different from your mother or father? In what ways are you alike?

3. When you were younger, what were some of the things that you did to bother your parents?

4. Did you or your family ever have a dangerous experience in which you came close to death?

There are some stories which my mother does not tell when there are men present: never at dinner, never at parties. She tells them to women only, usually in the kitchen, when they or we are helping with the dishes or shelling peas, or taking the tops and tails off the string beans, or husking corn. She tells them in a lowered voice, without moving her hands around in the air, and they contain no sound effects. These are stories of romantic betrayals, unwanted pregnancies, illnesses of various horrible kinds, marital infidelities, mental breakdowns, tragic suicides, unpleasant lingering deaths. They are not rich in detail or embroidered with incident: they are stark and factual. The women, their own hands moving among the dirty dishes or the husks of vegetables, nod solemnly.

Some of these stories, it is understood, are not to be passed on to my father, because they would upset him. It is well known that women can deal with this sort of thing better than men can. Men are not to be told anything they might find too painful; the secret depths of human nature, the sordid physicalities, might overwhelm or damage them. For instance, men often faint at the sight of their own blood, to which they are not accustomed. For this reason you should never stand behind one in the line at the Red Cross donor clinic. Men, for some mysterious reason, find life more difficult than women do. (My mother believes this, despite the female bodies, trapped, diseased, disappearing, or abandoned, that litter her stories.) Men must be allowed to play in the sandbox of their choice, as happily as they can, without disturbance; otherwise they get cranky and won't eat their dinners. There are all kinds of things that men are simply not equipped to understand, so why expect it of them? Not everyone shares this belief about men; nevertheless, it has its uses.

"She dug up the shrubs from around the house," says my mother. This story is about a shattered marriage: serious business. My mother's eyes widen. The other women lean forward. "All she left him were the shower curtains." There is a collective sigh, an expelling of breath. My father enters the kitchen, wondering when the tea will be ready, and the women close ranks, turning to him their deceptive blankly smiling faces. Soon afterwards, my mother emerges from the kitchen, carrying the tea pot, and sets it down on the table in its ritual place.

*   *   *

"I remember the time we almost died," says my mother. Many of her stories begin this way.

*   *   *

This is the story of the hay wagon. "Your father was driving," says my mother, "at the speed he usually goes." We read between the lines: *too fast.* "You kids were in the back." I can remember this day, so I can remember how old I was, how old my brother was. We were old enough to think it was funny to annoy my father by singing popular songs of a type he disliked, such as "Mockingbird Hill"; or perhaps we were imitating bagpipe music by holding our noses and humming, while hitting our Adam's apples with the edges of our hands. When we became too irritating my father would say, "Pipe down." We weren't old enough to know that his irritation could be real: we thought it was part of the game.

"We were going down a steep hill," my mother continues, "when a hay wagon pulled out right across the road, at the bottom. Your father put on the brakes, but nothing happened. The brakes were gone! I thought our last moment had come." Luckily the hay wagon continued across the road, and we shot past it, missing it by at least a foot. "My heart was in my mouth," says my mother.

Glossary

sound effects   special sounds that add emphasis in a conversation or presentation

romantic betrayals   disappointments in love

rich   complicated

close ranks   act together

read between the lines   understanding a meaning that is not written or said

Adam's apple   part of the front of the throat that moves up and down

pipe down   keep quiet

shot   moved quickly

Vocabulary _____

A. Find the word(s) closest in meaning to the underlined word. Circle the best answer.

1. The women were telling stories about <u>tragic</u> events.
   a. historical   b. very sad
   c. very interesting   d. exhilarating

2. They were afraid that the stories would <u>upset</u> men.
   a. disturb   b. excite   c. disappoint   d. change

3. They might feel <u>cranky</u> if they couldn't play in their sandbox.
   a. hurt   b. in a bad mood   c. in a good mood   d. idle

4. Their <u>deceptive</u> smiles made the father think that they were talking about happy things.
   a. delightful   b. guilty   c. remarkable   d. false

5. The women told stories that were <u>stark</u> and factual.
   a. detailed   b. colorful   c. mysterious   d. harsh

6. The children were making noise to <u>annoy</u> their father.
   a. fool   b. warn   c. leave   d. bother

7. The father found the noises <u>irritating</u>.
   a. soft   b. annoying   c. loud   d. normal

B. Complete the sentences with words from the list. A few words must be used more than once.

tragic	betrayals	upset	blankly
deceptive	suicides	deal with	solemnly
irritating		annoy	happily
romantic			luckily
horrible			

Many of my mother's stories were about _____ relationships in which someone was deceived. Other stories were about _____ illnesses and _____ breakdowns. The women nodded _____ when she spoke of _____ and _____. She told them about the hay wagon incident. _____, the story of the hay wagon did not have a _____ ending. Although the noises of the children were _____ to their father, they did not lead to a _____ result.

When the women were smiling _____ at her father, it was _____. They didn't want to _____ him. The women felt that men should not have to _____ painful incidents; they should be able to live as _____ as they can. Certain types of stories would _____ them.

Comprehension

1. What are the women doing when her mother tells the stories?
2. What kind of stories is her mother telling?
3. Why won't they tell these stories to her father?
4. What did the women believe about men?
5. Do you think the writer has the same beliefs as her mother? Tell why or why not.
6. Is there anything humorous about the incident told in paragraph three?
7. What did the mother think about the father's driving?
8. What were the children doing to irritate their father?
9. How do we know that the father was driving a car?
10. Why didn't the car hit the hay wagon?

Wordwork _____

CONNECTING IDEAS

Combine the sentences into one sentence using the connectives *nevertheless* or *otherwise*. Punctuate carefully. You may have to changes some nouns in the second sentence to pronouns.

EXAMPLE

The women smiled at my father. The women didn't tell him anything.

The women smiled at my father; nevertheless,
they didn't tell him anything.

1. Many women do not believe that men are so innocent. The idea is useful to them.

_____

_____

2. Men must not be upset by the painful secrets of human nature. Men might become unhappy and cranky.

_____

_____

3. Her mother always puts the teapot in the same place. Her husband might not look at her very happily.

_____

_____

4. Men should not look at their own blood. Men might faint.

_____

_____

5. My mother believes that men find life more difficult than women do. My mother's stories about women tell about their tragic lives.

_____

_____

6. The brakes of the car didn't work, and the car kept going. The car didn't hit the hay wagon.

_____

_____

7. The children didn't know that they were really irritating their father. The children probably would not have made those noises.

_____

_____

Never/Usually

The women usually tell their stories in the kitchen, and they never tell them when men are present.

1. List three things that you never do.

_____

_____

_____

2. List three things that you usually do in the kitchen.

_____

_____

_____

3. What are some things that you usually do not talk about to men? Why?

_____

_____

_____

4. What are some things that you usually do not talk about to women? Why?

_____

_____

_____

You Should Never

The writer refers to a situation which sounds funny: "You should never stand behind a man in the line at a Red Cross blood donor clinic."

1. Why shouldn't you? _____

2. Complete the following sentences with four different situations that you think are funny.

   a. You should never _____.

   b. You should never _____.

   c. You should never _____.

   d. You should never _____.

What Upsets Us

Most of us get upset at things, but what upsets us usually varies from individual to individual. What are some things that upset you? Complete as many of the items below as possible.

1. I am upset by _____.

2. My friends are always upset by _____.

3. My father is often upset by _____.

4. My teacher is upset by _____.

5. When I was younger, I used to upset my brothers and sisters by

   _____.

6. When I was younger, I used to upset my parents by _____

   _____.

Despite

Despite the tragic incidents that happened to women, the writer's mother believed that men find life more difficult than women do.

Complete the following sentences with your own ideas.

1. Despite my brother's noisy radio, I _____

   _____.

2. Despite all the people in the kitchen, she _____ _____ .

3. Despite his breakdown, his wife _____ _____ .

4. Despite having jobs in different cities, the couple _____ _____ .

5. Despite the blood on the knife, _____ _____ .

6. Despite _____ _____ .

Suggestions for Discussion and Writing _____

1. Describe a significant moment in the life of your mother or father.
2. Some newspapers and magazines specialize in stories of romantic betrayals, marital infidelities, and tragic deaths. Why do you think people read those stories?
3. What do you think is the author's attitude toward her mother? Does the author have the same beliefs?
4. Describe a dangerous experience that you have had.
5. Why does the mother begin her story about the hay wagon by saying, "I remember the time we almost died."?

Independent Study _____

1. Read another section of "Significant Moments in the Life of My Mother" in *Bluebeard's Egg*. Be prepared to report on it.
2. Read another short story by Atwood in one of her collections of short stories or read a section of one of her novels.
3. Look through newspapers and magazines to find a story that illustrates one of the following: marital infidelity, mental breakdown, romantic betrayal, unpleasant death, or a tragic accident. Be prepared to tell the story to the class.

4. Look up these words and be prepared to describe the differences in meaning: *serious, solemn, sober, grave, grim.*

5. Look up these words and be prepared to describe the differences in meaning: *disgust, enrage, annoy, irritate.*

6. The mother in the story says "My heart was in my mouth." Ask other people what they say to describe very dangerous moments. Find four different expressions.

3

The Last Escapade

Harry Mark Petrakis

Harry Mark Petrakis (b. 1923) is the author of eight novels and four collections of short stories. His latest novel, *A Ghost of the Sun*, continues the story of Leonidas Matsoukas, the hero of *A Dream of Kings*, which was made into a movie starring Anthony Quinn. Many of Petrakis' stories take place in the Greek-American community in Chicago and deal with universal themes such as aging, death, and the need for love.

"The Last Escapade" is a short story about the relationship between adults and their parents. The characters are Naomi, her brother Keith, and their 74-year old father. In the selection below, Naomi and Keith discuss their father's behavior, and then the father explains his actions to Keith.

PRE-READING QUESTIONS

1. In your country, do older parents usually live with their adult children or do they live by themselves?
2. Where did/do your grandparents live?
3. What did/do your grandparents do to keep busy?
4. Do you think a grandparent should marry again if his/her spouse dies?

"I'm ashamed to talk about it, even to you," his sister Naomi said. "But I'm at my wit's end about what I'm going to do with him. I had to phone you to come."

When he'd received her urgent message, he imagined it concerned their father, who was seventy-four and widowed six years since the death of his mother. He lived alone in an apartment a few miles from where Naomi lived with her husband and children. Several earlier conversations with his sister had hinted of his father's involvement with a girl. He had avoided talking to Naomi about it in the past but now he asked her if that was the problem.

"Not just a girl!" Naomi exclaimed. "A child! Keith, she's barely twenty years old! He met her . . . ," she lowered her voice so the children playing in another room would not hear, ". . . in a massage parlor!"

"Maybe he just wanted a massage," Keith said.

"Oh for God's sake, Keith, spare me your academic wit! This is the most dreadful crisis we have ever had with him!"

"After all, he's in pretty good health," Keith said. "Maybe he still has an active sex drive."

"I don't want to hear about his sex drive," she said. "I don't even want to think about what they do together! It's too disgusting! I'm sure he's giving her money and she hasn't any shame about cheating a senile old man."

"Are you sure he's giving her money?"

"He admitted it! A few times when I tried to talk to him about the danger of what he was doing, he grew impatient and flip with me and told me brazenly, he was paying her rent, gas and light!"

"That means she's not living with him."

"Oh God, don't even mention that possibility! If he did anything as stupid and outrageous as that I wouldn't let the children visit him again!"

"All right, Naomi," Keith tried to speak patiently. "He's seventy-four years old and he's involved with a twenty-year-old girl he met in a massage parlor. The whole business is a little sordid, I admit, but it seems to have been going on for some time. You mentioned it to me when I was here at Christmas. What makes it a crisis now?"

She rose from her chair and went to peer nervously into the dining room. The children had gone outside and she returned and sat down, leaning closer to speak to Keith in a shaken whisper.

"The girl had a baby two weeks ago!"
"Is he the father?" Keith asked.
"Don't be ridiculous!" Naomi said.

*   *   *

Keith couldn't become as agitated as Naomi but he understood her concern. His father lived on a pension from the Colony Insurance Company and his Social Security and didn't have to touch the money he'd received from the sale of their house when his mother died. Some of that money had gone to Naomi when she and Bruce bought their house and his father had given Keith ten thousand dollars while he studied for his doctoral degree. But there had to be seventy to eighty thousand dollars still in the bank. The money belonged to his father to do with as he wished, but they had a responsibility to make sure the girl didn't cheat him out of it.

"What do you think we should do?" Keith asked.

"You should go and talk to him," Naomi said sternly. "You are his son and maybe you men understand this kind of perversion. Try to make him understand that what he is doing is shameful and obscene!"

*   *   *

He phoned his father, who seemed delighted that Keith was in town and agreed to see him at once. He left Naomi's house after promising her he would return that evening to report to her exactly what his father had said.

*   *   *

"You know, son," his father said quietly, "I don't want to make excuses but the whole thing came about because of loneliness. I am not blaming your sister or you. You live four hundred miles away and she has her life with Bruce and her children. But when a man is alone as he grows older, you have to understand that his days and nights are different. He doesn't have the expectations he had when he was young, or the dreams, or planning for the things he hopes to do. He wakes up in the silence of the dark room and can't help thinking that it's just another night moving him closer to death. Oh, I know, there is the senior center nearby and movies and television. But I find that gathering of old people depressing and television is full of idiotic comedies and the movies show films that have nothing to do with the life I lived. I am grateful when you and Naomi and the children and I enjoy holidays and birthdays. But those celebrations pass quickly and then there are empty, lonely weeks again." His father shrugged. "I said I didn't want to make excuses but I guess I just did."

Glossary

at my wit's end not knowing what to do

involvement being part of a situation

massage parlor a place for massages or for prostitution

had to be must be

came about resulted

Vocabulary

A. Find the word(s) closest in meaning to the underlined word. Circle the best answer.

1. Naomi thought that her father's involvement with a young girl was outrageous.
   a. shocking b. expensive c. pleasing d. active

2. Naomi didn't realize that her father's life could be very depressing.
   a. sad b. unhealthy c. lonely d. exciting

3. Keith's father spoke brazenly about his relationship with the young girl.
   a. quietly   b. secretly
   c. without honor   d. without shame

4. Naomi thought that her father had become a senile old man.
   a. intelligent   b. impatient
   c. losing his wife   d. losing his mind

5. Naomi felt that her father's behavior with the young girl was sordid.
   a. dumb b. indecent c. illegal d. clever

B. Complete the sentences with words from the list.

lonely   involvement   enjoy
senile   wit   avoid
disgusting   expectations   cheat
depressing
impatient

Naomi thought that her father's _____ with a young girl showed that he was _____. She felt that her father's behavior was _____, and she was afraid that the girl might _____ him. When Keith suggested that his father only wanted a massage at the massage parlor, Naomi became _____ with Keith's _____. Her father, however, was simply _____. He wanted to _____ the _____ life at the senior centers. He didn't have any _____ for the future, and he wanted to _____ the time that he had.

Comprehension

1. Where did Naomi's father live?
2. How old was Naomi's father?
3. How old was the girl?
4. How did Naomi feel about her father's involvement with the girl?
5. How did Keith react to Naomi's news about their father?
6. What did Keith do when he heard the news?
7. What did Keith's father tell him?
8. Who was the father of the girl's baby?
9. Naomi and Keith were both concerned about their father's behavior, but they were worried about different things. What was Naomi worried about? What was Keith worried about?
10. Do you think the father wanted to live with Naomi or Keith? Why?

Wordwork _____

CONNECTING IDEAS

Combine the sentences into one sentence using the word *that*. You may have to change some nouns in the second sentence to pronouns. Study the example.

EXAMPLE

My father smiled at the women. He saw the women in the kitchen.

My father smiled at the women
_____

that he saw in the kitchen.
_____

1. He didn't have to use the money. He received the money from the sale of a house.

_____

_____

2. Keith used the money to pay for his education. His father gave Keith money.

_____

_____

3. When he was young, he planned for things. He hoped to do things.

_____

_____

4. Naomi didn't like the girl. Her father was helping the girl.

_____

_____

5. The father lived on a pension. The father got the pension from the Colony Insurance Company.

_____

_____

6. He was paying the rent for a girl. He met the girl in a massage parlor.

_____

_____

What Am I Going to Do With . . . ?

Describe the problem that makes you ask the following questions. The first one is done for you.

1. What am I going to do with my cats?

   They are bringing mice in the house.

2. What am I going to do with my dog?

   _____

3. What am I going to do with my teenager?

   _____

4. What am I going to do with you?

   _____

5. What am I going to do with my mother?

   _____

6. What am I going to do with my girlfriend?

   _____

Lower Your Voice

1. Complete the following sentences by describing situations in which someone lowered his or her voice. The first one is done for you.

   a. My father lowered his voice when he _was talking to my mother about_

   financial problems.

   b. The students lowered their voices when the teacher _____

   _____

   c. My sister lowered her voice when I _____

   _____

d. I was talking on the telephone, but I lowered my voice when my roommate _____

_____

e. The girls in the library lowered their voices when _____

_____

2. Why did they lower their voices?

a. The girls lowered their voices because _____

_____

b. I lowered my voice so that my roommate _____

_____

c. My sister lowered her voice so that _____

_____

d. My father lowered his voice because _____

_____

e. The students lowered their voices because _____

_____

Suggestions for Discussion and Writing _____

1. Where do you think parents or grandparents should live when they are old?
2. What are the responsibilities of children for their parents?
3. What do you think of the relationship between Naomi's father and the girl?
4. Which character in this story do you like best? Why?
5. Do you agree or disagree with Naomi's ideas?
6. Describe a family you know in which differences between older and younger people have created problems.

Independent Study

1. Find out what happens at the end of "The Last Escapade."
2. Find out what the "sandwich generation" means. Is Naomi a member of the sandwich generation? Is Keith?
3. Look up these words and be prepared to describe the differences in meaning: *elderly, ancient, senile, doddering, no chicken.*
4. Look up these words and be prepared to describe the differences in meaning: *sordid, obscene, shameful, perverse.*
5. What do you think Keith told Naomi about his meeting with their father? Write the telephone conversation that might have taken place.
6. Go to the library and find an article on the problems of the elderly in the United States. Does a similar situation exist in your country?
7. What are the advantages and disadvantages of having large extended families where the parents, children, and grandparents all live together?

Review

1. Do you think the women in "Significant Moments in the Life of My Mother" would be upset about Naomi's father? How would she react?

2. The three selections in this unit present various aspects of family life. Which seem most familiar to you? Which seems most strange?

3. In some countries there are special days for family members, such as Mother's Day and Father's Day. Why do you think such days may have become popular? In what other ways do people honor family members?

4. There is a saying in English, "You can choose your friends but you can't choose your relatives." What is the significance of that saying?

5. Which of the three writers in this unit is the easiest to read? Which writer is the hardest to read? Why?

6. Relationships between parents and children are a good source of material for writers. If you were going to write about a parent-child relationship, what would you write about?

7. What books about relationships written in your native language would you recommend?

UNIT THREE
Mysteries

UNIT INTRODUCTION

Mystery stories have always been very popular. These stories usually involve dangerous situations or a sudden death. They are generally about crime and suspense. The reader often has the challenge of trying to decide what has happened or is going to happen. Frequently, the end of the story is a surprise. And often the end of the story is also ironic. What happens is the opposite of what we expected to happen. These characteristics make mystery stories interesting. The first story in this unit, "A Case for the UN," presents us with a murder and a surprise ending that makes us think. The second story, "Drum Beat," involves a danger to the lives of the passengers on an airplane and then a surprise solution that depends on a clue, one important detail. Although the final story, "Death Speaks," is not like the other two, it combines the threat of death, a surprise ending, and irony.

UNIT PRE-READING

1. Do you like mystery stories? Why or why not?

2. Think of a mystery story in which one clue was very important.

3. Do you like surprise endings?

4. Can you think of a frightening situation in which you finally felt relief?

1

A Case for the UN

Miriam Allen de Ford

Miriam Allen de Ford (1888–1975) was an American writer whose stories, poems, and articles appeared in magazines and anthologies. She won many poetry prizes as well as awards for her mystery stories. Many of her mystery stories were sold to radio and television.

The mystery story is a very popular form of fiction today. Each story usually has a murder, a detective who is the hero or heroine, and an unexpected ending. The selection below is taken from a story called "A Case for the UN," which was written in 1964. In this story, a plane is flying over the Atlantic Ocean from New York to Shannon, the international airport in Ireland. The name of the pilot is Kemper and Mavis is one of the flight attendants.

PRE-READING QUESTIONS

1. What are the responsibilities of an airplane pilot?

2. What authority does a pilot have over the people on the plane? What can he make the passengers do? What *can't* he make the passengers do?

3. When you are flying in a plane, over the Atlantic or over the Pacific ocean, which country are you in? Whose laws do you obey or disobey?

At three o'clock in the morning they were over the mid-Atlantic.

It was then that the little man in the rear, Bartholomew Evans, got quietly to his feet. No one paid any attention to him; others had arisen from time to time and gone back to the lavatory.

Evans stepped forward silently until he stood in the aisle between Renée Blanc and Giuseppe Falconari, who were now sound asleep, their heads buried in pillows.

Very calmly and deliberately, Evans drew a pistol from his pocket, and shot each of them through the head.

Immediately there was pandemonium. Startled passengers awoke, jumped up, cried out. Mavis ran to the cockpit, forgetting her shoes, and almost collided with Kemper as he opened the door and hurried to the scene.

The murderer made no attempt to move. He stood there with the smoking pistol still in his hand. Not a sound came from either of his victims; there was not even much blood. Both had been killed instantly.

The pilot took command at once.

"Please resume your seats," Kemper ordered, hoping his voice was steady. He had heard plenty of stories of sensational events on other planes, but this was his first and, he hoped, his last experience of this kind. "See to this lady," he added to Mavis; an elderly woman sitting nearby was in hysterics. Mavis, her legs trembling, ministered to the woman and got her quieted down. There was little noise otherwise; most of the passengers were too shocked to speak.

A heavy-set man stood up and started toward the murderer. Kemper stopped him with a gesture. The responsibility and the danger — were his.

"Give me the gun," he demanded of Evans.

The coolest person on board was the murderer.

"Certainly, Captain," Evans replied politely, placing the gun in Kemper's outstretched hand. "And you needn't tie me up. I'm not going to pull any doors open and jump out, or do anything foolish."

Unexpectedly somebody laughed. Someone else reached blindly for a paper bag and was sick in it.

"Ladies and gentlemen, please keep your seats," the pilot said, his voice steady now. "I know how distressing this must be for you, but there is nothing we can do until we arrive at Shannon.

Mavis, I think everybody could use a drink. But first get some blankets to cover these—these two people. And if you, madam, and you, sir, who were sitting next to them would find places elsewhere—"

The suggestion was unnecessary; the victims' neighbors were already hunched in seats farther away.

"Now"—Kemper turned to the still unmoving Evans—"I shall have you placed under guard until I can turn you over to the Eire authorities when we land. Our copilot will have wired ahead, and the police will have been notified. They'll be waiting for you. Now, if two of you gentlemen will volunteer to keep an eye on him—"

The burly man and another stepped forward.

Bartholomew Evans smiled.

"You know, Captain," he said conversationally, "I happen to be a lawyer, and I know a few things that you don't. For instance, though an aircraft in flight has the legal status of a ship at sea, its pilot does not have the power of arrest and detention that a ship's captain has. You have no right whatever to hold or guard me.

"And the authorities you say will be waiting to apprehend me can do nothing whatever. Eire has no jurisdiction over me. I waited deliberately to do my—deed until we were over the mid-Atlantic. My whole action depended on the fact that no nation in the world has jurisdiction in this matter. I've made very sure of the law. There is *nowhere* I can be held, *nowhere* I can be tried. There is no such thing as a code of international criminal air law, nor is there any Air Police Force."

Glossary _____

sound asleep   sleeping deeply

see to (someone)   help

at once   immediately

keep your seats   remain in your seats

turn you over   give you

Eire   Irish (Gaelic word)

keep an eye on   watch

be tried   have a trial

Vocabulary

A. Find the word(s) closest in meaning to the underlined word. Circle the best answer.

1. The passengers were <u>shocked</u> when they saw the man fire a pistol.
   a. sad   b. very surprised   c. frightened   d. relieved

2. He raised his gun and <u>deliberately</u> fired two shots.
   a. quickly and casually   b. high in the air
   c. slowly and carefully   d. with two hands

3. Of all the people on the plane, the killer was the <u>coolest</u>.
   a. least nervous   b. least happy
   c. most happy   d. most nervous

4. After the man fired his gun, there was <u>pandemonium</u> on the airplane.
   a. silence and fear   b. bells and sirens
   c. noise and confusion   d. smoke and fire

5. The question was who has <u>jurisdiction</u> when a crime is committed over the ocean.
   a. justice   b. motivation   c. hysterics   d. authority

B. Complete the sentences with words from the list.

hysterics	resume	sound
shots	see to	shocked
	jumped up	

When the _____shots_____ sounded, most of the passengers were

_____sound_____ asleep. The stewardess _____jumped up_____ from her seat and

ran to the cockpit. The pilot told her to _____see to_____ an old woman

who was in _____hysterics_____. The pilot then told the passengers to

_____resume_____ their seats. Most of the passengers were too

_____shocked_____ to speak.

awoke   foolish   deliberately
depend on   shocked   quietly
started   calmly
volunteer

A man said to Evans, "I ___*awoke*___ when you ___*started*___ to walk ___*quietly*___ down the aisle of the plane. You took your gun out ___*calmly*___ and shot those people ___*deliberately*___. You are ___*foolish*___ if you think you can ___*depend on*___ a legal technicality to escape. I am ___*shocked*___ at your act and I will ___*volunteer*___ my help to the police."

Comprehension

1. At what time did the murder happen?
2. Where was the plane at the time of the murder?
3. Who was watching Evans?
4. Where had Evans been sitting?
5. How did Evans kill the couple?
6. What was the couple doing when Evans killed them?
7. How did the passengers react when they heard the shots?
8. What did the flight attendant do?
9. What did Evans do?
10. Who took command? What did he do?
11. Who did Mavis help? Why?
12. Why wasn't there much noise on the plane?
13. How did the pilot get the gun from the murderer?
14. Did the Captain tie Evans up?
15. What did the pilot tell the passengers to do?
16. What did the pilot tell Mavis to do?
17. What did the pilot intend to do with the murderer?
18. Was Evans worried about being arrested? Why?
19. Why did the murderer wait until the plane was over the Atlantic before he killed his victims?
20. Do you think the story ends with Evans' speech? Why or why not?

Wordwork _____

CONNECTING IDEAS

The following sentences are not in the best order. Rearrange the sentences in an order that shows how the ideas are connected and write your sentences below. You may change nouns to pronouns and combine sentences.

1. At that moment he stood up. She started to walk toward him. He looked innocent. When she returned to the cabin, she looked at the man in the rear seat. He was a middle-aged man with glasses. He was reading a newspaper.

   _____

   _____

   _____

   _____

   _____

   _____

2. There was pandemonium. The man shot two passengers. He walked over to two sleeping passengers. The murderer made no attempt to move. The man walked up the aisle.

   _____

   _____

   _____

   _____

   _____

   _____

3. The pilot took command at once. The murderer said that no country had jurisdiction over him. A burly man volunteered to guard the murderer. The pilot demanded the gun from the murderer. The flight attendant quieted down a hysterical woman.

_____

_____

_____

_____

_____

_____

Reaction to Fear

People react to fear in different ways.

1. How did the passengers on the plane react to fear?

_____

_____

2. What are some other things people do when they are afraid?

_____

_____

3. What do you do when you are afraid? Describe one time when you were afraid.

_____

_____

Too _____ to Do It

"Most of the passengers were too *shocked* to speak." What other adjectives could you use in that phrase (too _____ to _____) to describe the reactions of the passengers, pilot, and flight attendants. Write your own sentence for number 5.

1. They were too _____.

2. The pilot was too _____.

3. The flight attendants were too _____.

4. The other passengers were too _____.

5. _____

Varying the Theme

1. What could have happened if the pilot had not taken command at once?

   _____

   _____

2. What could have happened if the victims had awakened before the man fired?

   _____

   _____

3. What could have happened if the murderer had not been cool?

   _____

   _____

4. What would have happened if this were a James Bond movie?

   _____

   _____

Puzzles and Mysteries

Many detective stories make the readers think of different solutions. Here are a few puzzles for you to try.

1. John weighed 198 pounds. He was walking along the road carrying three coconuts. Each coconut weighed one pound. He came to a bridge and saw a sign there. The sign read: This bridge can support only 200 pounds. How did John get across the bridge in one trip with his three coconuts?

2. There was a man who had to take a wolf, a goat, and a cabbage across a river. His boat was very small; it would hold only the man and *one other thing*. What could the man do? How could he take the wolf, the goat, and the cabbage across the river, one at a time, so that the wolf wouldn't eat the goat and the goat wouldn't eat the cabbage?

   (Hint: First, the man took the goat across.)

   (For the answers, see page 193.)

Suggestions for Discussion and Writing _____

1. Describe the most frightening experience you have had on an airplane or on any other means of transportation.
2. Most airports now have security systems. Do you think they are effective? Do you have any suggestions for improvement?
3. Do you know of any situation in which a guilty person was not punished because of a law or a conflict between laws?
4. What is the penalty for murder in your country? Compare that penalty with penalties in other countries.

Independent Study

1. This selection is not the complete story; it has an ending. What do you think happened at the end of the story? Write your own ending. Then look at page 193 and compare your ending with the author's ending.

2. Find out what power and authority the United Nations has now. Describe one situation in which the UN used its authority. Support your paper with references if possible.

3. Look up the Miranda vs. Arizona case. Why did the United States Supreme Court reverse an Arizona conviction? What are Miranda warnings?

4. Look up these words and be prepared to describe the differences in meaning: *pandemonium, frenzy, turmoil, riot, uproar, hullabaloo.*

5. Non-sexist words have replaced many words that indicated the sex of a person. For example, flight attendant has replaced steward and stewardess. What are some other examples of non-sexist language? What words are commonly used instead of:

    a. salesman   _____

    b. mailman   _____

    c. foreman   _____

    d. chairman   _____

    e. policeman   _____

    f. weatherman   _____

    g. fireman   _____

2

Drum Beat

Stephen Marlowe

Stephen Marlowe (b. 1928) has written science fiction and crime novels under several names including Adam Chase, Andrew Frazer, Jason Ridgeway, and Milton Lesser (his original name). He has also published two novels: *1956: a novel* and *The Memoirs of Christopher Columbus.*

Marlowe has written a series of stories involving a private investigator named Chester (Chet) Drum. "Drum Beat" is about a man named Sam Heyn, who is going to Washington, D.C. on a plane. He is going to talk to a committee of the United States Congress about the Trucker's Brotherhood, a union in the Midwestern part of the United States. He probably has information that some people in the union do not want anyone to know about. The narrator is Drum.

PRE-READING QUESTIONS

1. Why do people hire private investigators?

2. What do you think is the most dangerous thing that could happen on a plane flight?

3. Have you read any stories about bombs on airplanes?

4. What do shiny black cars make you think of?

The big man sitting next to me in the window seat of the turboprop that was flying from Duluth, Minnesota, to Washington, D.C., looked at his watch and said, "Ten after seven, Drum. We're halfway there. If I were running away and out over the ocean somewhere, they'd call it the point of no return."

"You're not running away, Mr. Heyn," I said.

He smiled a little and agreed. "No, I'm not running away."

And then the ticking started.

Heyn's eyes widened. He'd been living with uncertainty and fear too long. The physical response was instant: the widening of the eyes, the sudden rictus of the mouth, a hand clutching at my wrist on the armrest between us.

The wordless response said: You read the papers, don't you? This wouldn't be the first bomb planted aboard an air liner, would it? And I'm a marked man, you know I am. That's why you're here.

I stood up quite calmly, but a pulse had begun to hammer in my throat, as if in time to the ticking. For a moment I saw the deep blue of the sky beyond Heyn's head and then on the luggage rack over it I saw the attaché case. It wasn't Sam Heyn's. Heyn's was next to it, monogrammed.

The ticking came from the unmarked case. It was very loud, or maybe that was my imagination. It sounded almost like a drum — each beat drumming our lives away and the lives of forty other innocent people in the turboprop.

I looked at the attaché case. I didn't touch it. Time-rigged, sure; but who could tell what kind of a spit-and-string mechanism activated it? Maybe just lifting it from the rack would set it off.

A minute had passed. Heyn asked, "Find it?"

I nodded mutely. A little boy squirmed around in the seat in front of Heyn. "Mommy," he said. "I hear a clock."

Mommy heard it too. She gave Heyn and me a funny look. Just then a stewardess came by with a tray. She stopped in the aisle next to my seat, in a listening attitude.

"Is that yours?" Her smile was strained. "With a clock in it, I hope?"

"It's not mine." I squeezed near her in the narrow aisle. Close to her ear I said softly, "It may be a bomb, miss. That's Sam Heyn in the window seat."

Her back stiffened. That was all. Then she hurried forward to the pilot's compartment. Heyn looked at me. A moment later over the PA a man's voice said:

"Whoever owns the unmarked attaché case above seat seventeen, please claim it. This is the captain speaking. Whoever owns . . ."

I heard the ticking that was like a drum. Faces turned. There was talking in the cabin of the turboprop. No one claimed the attaché case.

Sweat beaded Heyn's forehead. "When, dammit?" he said. "When will it go off?"

The captain came back. He had one of those self-confident, impassive faces they all have. He looked at the attaché case and listened to it. A man across the aisle got up to speak to him.

"Sit down, please," the captain said.

Then a voice said: "Bomb . . ." and the passengers scrambled from their seats toward the front and rear of the cabin. In the confusion I told the captain quickly, "My name is Chet Drum. I'm a private investigator bringing Sam Heyn here to testify in Washington before the Hartsell Committee. If he can prove what the Truckers' Brotherhood's been up to in the Midwest, there's going to be trouble."

"I can prove it," Heyn muttered.

I stared at the attaché case. I heard the ticking. It didn't look as if he'd get the chance.

"We could unload it out the door," the captain told me.

"Cabin's pressurized, isn't it?"

"So?"

"Who the hell knows how it's rigged? Change of pressure could be enough to set it off."

The captain nodded. He raised his voice and shouted, "Will you please all resume your seats?" Then he said, "If we could land in a hurry . . ." His face brightened. "Jesus, wait a minute." He looked at his watch. "Seven-nineteen," he said. Nine minutes had passed since the ticking started. "All we need is four thousand feet of runway. There's a small airport near New Albany . . ."

He rushed forward. Seconds later we were told to fasten our seat belts for an emergency landing. The big turboprop whined into a steep glide.

The attaché case ticked and ticked.

We came in twice. The first time the wind was wrong, and the captain had to try it again. Buzzing the field, I saw a windsock tower, two small lonely hangars and three shiny black cars waiting on the apron of the runway.

Three black cars waiting for what?

I felt my facial muscles relax. I smiled idiotically at Sam Heyn. He frowned back at me, mopping sweat from his forehead. "Well, well, well," I said.

He almost jumped from his seat when I reached over his head and lifted down the ticking attaché case. The man across the aisle gasped. We were banking steeply for our second run at the field. I carried the attaché case forward and through the door to the crew compartment.

The copilot had the stick. The captain looked at me and the attaché case. "Are you nuts or something?"

"I almost was."

He just stared. The flaps were down. We were gliding in.

"Keep away from that field," I said. The copilot ignored me.

I did the only thing I could to make them listen. I smashed the attaché case against a bulkhead, breaking the lock. The captain had made a grab for me, missing. I opened the case. There was a quiet little clock inside, and a noisy big one. The little one had triggered the big one to start at seven-ten. That was all.

No bomb.

"They knew your route," I said. "They figured you wouldn't dare ditch a time bomb, knew you'd have to land here if you heard it ticking at seven-ten. Three shiny black cars waiting at an airport in the middle of nowhere. They're waiting for Heyn." I pointed. "If you radio down below, you can have them picked up by the cops."

It was seven-thirty. "I never want to live through another twenty minutes like that," the captain said.

Neither did I. But Sam Heyn would get to Washington on schedule.

Glossary

point of no return   a moment on a trip when you are closer to the place that you are going to than the place you are coming from

rictus opening

planted hidden

marked man   a person targeted for harm

time-rigged   planned, usually through a mechanism, to happen at a certain time

spit-and-string   made with simple things, such as string, and may not last a long time

dammit   damn it

buzzing   flying over a place, usually at a low altitude

Vocabulary _____

A. Find the word(s) closest in meaning to the underlined word(s). Circle the best answer.

1. The little boy heard something ticking inside the attaché case.
    a. making a noise like a clock   b. making a noise like a mosquito
    c. making a noise like a bell   d. making a noise like a bee

2. It was possible that a change of pressure could set off the bomb.
    a. damage   b. drop   c. explode   d. raise

3. Chet figured that a small airfield would not usually have three shiny black cars on it.
    a. agreed   b. feared   c. said   d. concluded

4. The pilot told the passengers to fasten their seat belts because there was an emergency.
    a. an expected and safe event   b. an unexpected and safe event
    c. an expected and dangerous event   d. an unexpected and dangerous event

5. Although there was the danger of a bomb, the pilot's face was impassive.
    a. red   b. showing feelings
    c. pale   d. showing no feelings

B. Complete the sentences with words from the list. Some words may be used more than once.

activate	smiled	sweat	bomb
smile	stiffened	pulse	tick
	smashed	drum	fear
	frowned		

When Chet first heard the _____ of the clock, his

_____ began to beat quickly. Sam couldn't _____, his

eyes widened, and his hand _____. You could see the

_____ on his face. They didn't know what could

_____ the bomb. Soon the ticking began to sound like a

_____. Everyone became nervous, and _____ appeared

on Sam's forehead.

When Chet realized what was happening at the airport, he looked

at Sam and _____. Sam _____ at Chet. Then Chet

took the attaché case and _____ it against the wall. He knew

that it wasn't a _____.

Comprehension

1. Who was Sam Heyn?
2. Who was Chet Drum?
3. Where was the ticking coming from?
4. What did the Captain want to do with the attaché case?
5. What did Chet tell the Captain about the Captain's idea?
6. What did the Captain decide to do?
7. What did Chet notice about the airfield?
8. What did Chet do to the attaché case? Why?
9. What were the black cars doing there?
10. Why were they lucky that the wind was blowing the wrong way?

Wordwork

CONNECTING IDEAS

Combine each pair of sentences into one sentence. You may change nouns to pronouns.

EXAMPLE

The big man was sitting next to me. The big man looked at his watch.

_____ *The big man sitting next to me looked at his watch.* _____

1. The flight attendant was walking by with a tray. The flight attendant heard the ticking noise.

   _____

   _____

2. The man is going to Washington on the plane. The man is planning to talk to a Congressional committee.

   _____

   _____

3. The cars were waiting on the runway. The cars were shiny and black.

   _____

   _____

4. The sound was coming from the attaché case. The sound could have been a ticking bomb.

   _____

   _____

5. A man was sitting across the aisle. A man got up to speak to the captain.

   _____

   _____

Flying

Describe a time when you or someone you know had a moment of fear at an airport or while flying.

_____

_____

_____

_____

_____

_____

Noises

There are many different words to describe the noises made by different things. For example, a clock may tick. An alarm clock may ring. Below, write a sound made by the items on the list. There are several possibilities for each.

1. A plane may _____.

2. A mouse may _____.

3. A door may _____.

4. A person sleeping may _____.

5. Fingers may _____.

6. A drum may _____.

7. A stereo may _____.

8. A dry cereal may _____.

9. A mosquito may _____.

10. Your choice: _____.

A Funny Look

Very often a strange look on someone's face can tell us something important. Describe a situation in which a funny look was important.

EXAMPLE

When I asked my guest if he wanted a hot dog, my wife gave me

a funny look. I didn't know that my guest didn't eat meat.

_____

_____

_____

_____

_____

Murder Is My Business

Marlowe's series of Chester Drum stories have such titles as:
   Trouble is My Name
   Killers are My Meat
   Homicide is My Game
   Jeopardy is My Job
   Danger is My Line

Using the same pattern, make a list of some titles for mystery stories that you may someday write.

_____

_____

_____

_____

_____

Suggestions for Discussion and Writing

1. Why is the story called "Drum Beat"?
2. Who is the hero of the story? How does the author show us that this person is the hero?
3. What were the most important details in the story? Why?
4. Was there anything in the story that you didn't understand? If so, what didn't the author tell you?

Independent Study

1. Read another Chet Drum mystery story and be prepared to tell it to the class.
2. Look at a map and find out where the point of no return would be if you were flying from Tokyo to San Francisco; from Caracas to Montreal; from Nairobi to Frankfort.
3. Make two columns, one with the word *quiet* over it, one with the word *noisy* over it. Then check the meaning of the following words and put them in the column where you think they belong: *thunder, alarm, whisper, explode, sigh, mutter, whine, mutely, smash, hammer, hush, muffle.*
4. Write a brief description of a time in your life that was very quiet or very noisy.

3

Death Speaks

W. Somerset Maugham

Somerset Maugham (1874–1965) was a writer for most of his life. His stories, novels, and plays have become popular throughout the world, and many of his stories have been turned into films. Among his best known novels are *Of Human Bondage* and *Moon and Sixpence*. Some of Maugham's best works can be found in his *Collected Short Stories* and *Collected Plays*.

The following story comes from the play *Sheppey*. It involves death, a surprise ending, and irony, and it reminds us of ghost stories (stories of the supernatural). Some of the language is old-fashioned: the word *provisions* instead of *food*, for example. Some of the language is more formal than usual: "I will avoid my fate." The author also has not put punctuation marks where we would expect them. The title "Death Speaks" means that Death, who is a woman here, is telling the story. The words *I* and *me* at the end of the story refer to Death.

PRE-READING QUESTIONS

1. When people want to show the idea of death in your country, as a person or as a symbol, how do they do it?

2. Do you know any stories in which Death appears as a person?

3. What does the idea of fate mean to you?

There was a merchant in Bagdad who sent his servant to market to buy provisions and in a little while the servant came back, white and trembling, and said, Master, just now when I was in the market-place I was jostled by a woman in the crowd and when I turned I saw it was Death that jostled me. She looked at me and made a threatening gesture; now, lend me your horse, and I will ride away from this city and avoid my fate. I will go to Samarra and there Death will not find me. The merchant lent him his horse, and the servant mounted it, and he dug his spurs in its flanks and as fast as the horse could gallop he went. Then the merchant went down to the market-place and he saw me standing in the crowd and he came to me and said, Why did you make a threatening gesture to my servant when you saw him this morning? That was not a threatening gesture, I said, it was only a start of surprise. I was astonished to see him in Bagdad, for I had an appointment with him tonight in Samarra.

Glossary

to market to the market

Master a form of address that was used by servants

Samarra a town in Iraq, about 65 miles northwest of Bagdad

start a sudden movement (used as a noun here)

Vocabulary

A. Find the word(s) closest in meaning to the underlined word. Circle the best answer.

1. When the servant returned from the marketplace, he was pale and trembling.
   a. smiling   b. shaking   c. crying   d. talking

2. The marketplace was crowded, and Death jostled the servant there.
   a. met   b. threatened   c. pushed   d. hit

3. The servant tried to avoid Death by going to Samarra.
   a. escape   b. save   c. meet   d. destroy

4. Death said that she was <u>astonished</u> that the servant had been in the marketplace.
   a. pleased   b. angry   c. unhappy   d. surprised

B. Complete the sentences with words from the list. A few words must be used more than once.

gesture	lend	trembling
servant	avoid	astonished
Death		threatening
appointment		
marketplace		

There once was a _____ in Baghdad who worked for a merchant. One day the servant was in the _____. He saw a woman make a _____ towards him, and he knew that the woman was _____. The servant returned home _____ and asked the merchant to _____ him a horse. He wanted to leave Baghdad and go to Samarra so that he could _____ Death.

The merchant went to the _____ and asked Death why she had made a _____ gesture to his _____. Death said that she was _____ to have seen the servant in the marketplace in the morning because she had an _____ with him in Samarra that evening.

Comprehension _____

1. Who went to the market?
2. Why did he go?
3. How did the servant look when he came back?
4. What did a woman in the crowd do?
5. Who was the woman?
6. What kind of gesture did the woman make?

7. What did the servant ask his master?

8. Why did the servant want to leave the city?

9. Why did the servant want to go to Samarra?

10. How did the merchant help the servant?

11. Where did the merchant go?

12. Who did he see in the crowd?

13. What did he say to Death?

14. Did Death say she had made a threatening gesture?

15. Why was Death surprised?

Wordwork

CONNECTING IDEAS

The following sentences are not in the best order. Rearrange the sentences in an order that shows how the ideas are connected and then write the sentences below. You may change nouns to pronouns, combine sentences, and make other changes to make the paragraph flow smoothly.

He told the merchant that a woman had pushed him. He had a servant. The servant came back soon. A merchant lived in Baghdad. He sent the servant to the market. He said that the woman was Death. He wanted the servant to get some food.

_____

_____

_____

_____

_____

_____

_____

_____

Gestures

The servant thought that Death made a threatening gesture to him.

1. What kind of gesture do you think Death made?
2. How would you make a threatening gesture?
3. What gestures would you use for:
   a. Hello.
   b. I've made a mistake.
   c. Goodbye.
   d. It's hot.
   e. Come here.
   f. It's wonderful.
   g. I don't know.
   h. Good luck.
   i. He's crazy.
   j. What did you say?
   k. It's cold.
   l. I don't believe it.

Fate

Many people throughout the world believe in fate, but this belief appears in different ways in different places.

There are sayings that show a belief in fate. For example, in English:
When it's your time to go, it's your time to go.
That's life.
That's the way the ball bounces.
You have to take the bitter with the sweet.

1. If there are sayings about fate in your culture, translate them and write a few of them below.

   _____

   _____

   _____

2. Are there songs or stories in your culture that have examples of the idea of fate? Describe one briefly below.

   _____

   _____

   _____

Varying the Theme

A. Imagine that the story was different. What could have happened?

EXAMPLE

There was a lot of food in the merchant's house.

_____*He wouldn't send his servant to the marketplace.*_____

1. The merchant didn't have a horse.

_____

2. There was no crowd in the marketplace.

_____

3. The servant was blind.

_____

4. Death was a man.

_____

B. The ending of the story is not a happy one. Can you think of another possible ending? How would the story end in a Hollywood movie?

_____

_____

_____

_____

Personification

1. Death appears as a woman in this story. Does Death appear frequently as a person nowadays? How is it represented?

_____

_____

2. What other ideas are personified (appear as persons)? The Statue of Liberty, for example, is a woman who personifies the idea of liberty. Write a few examples below.

_____

_____

_____

Suggestions for Discussion and Writing _____

1. Retell the story.
2. Describe an incident in which someone avoided death.
3. Describe an incident in which someone didn't avoid death.
4. Describe an incident that was ironic.
5. Describe a situation in which gestures are important. Include an example of a situation in which not knowing a gesture can lead to a problem in communication.

Independent Study _____

1. Read a short story by W. Somerset Maugham and be prepared to tell the story to the class.
2. Read a short story by John O'Hara or another well-known short story writer and be prepared to tell the story to the class.
3. Look up the book *Handbook of Gestures* by Robert Saitz and Edward Cervenka. Read a section that interests you. Be ready to tell the class about it.
4. One of Maugham's most famous quotations is "I've always been interested in people, but I don't like them." Find another quotation attributed to Maugham.
5. Look up the differences in meaning between these pairs of words: *lend/ borrow; come/go; bring/take.*

Review

1. Suppose Chet Drum had been on the same plane as Evans. Do you think he could have prevented the murder? Would he have taken charge afterwards? What would he have done?

2. Make up a story in which Death is on an airplane.

3. In "A Case for the UN" and "Drum Beat," the authors introduce a dramatic event near the beginning of the stories. What are those events? Why do the authors do that? They both also have a surprise toward the end. What are the surprises?

4. Who are some well-known mystery writers in your country?

5. What is your favorite mystery story? Why?

6. Who are Edgar Allen Poe, Inspector Clouseau, Alfred Hitchcock, Atropos, and the Angel of Death? Why might we think of these people when we read this unit?

7. Bram Stoker and Mary Shelley were writers who created well-known monsters. What were the names of the books and some of the movies that have been made based on the books?

8. Which story in this unit did you like the best? Why?

UNIT FOUR
Going Places

UNIT INTRODUCTION

In this unit, the writers express a common feeling—that we all would like to leave our ordinary lives and go somewhere else where everything will be better. We often think that we can solve our problems by going away, to someplace new and different. Of course, sometimes it works and sometimes it doesn't. In "How My Love Was Sawed in Half," a young boy dreams of living in a world that is different from the ordinary world of his family. In "Estelle," a young girl is bored with her life in a small town and leaves for the excitement of a big city. And in "Jones Beach," the writer describes a day when he decides to stop what he is doing and simply drive away to get a feeling of freedom.

UNIT PRE-READING

1. Do you know people who are unhappy where they are living?

2. Do you have dreams of your future? Where do those dreams take you?

3. What do you do when you need to get away by yourself for a while? Where do you go?

4. If you were asked to imagine a perfect place, what would it look like?

1

How My Love Was Sawed in Half

Robert Fontaine

Robert Fontaine (1913–1965) was a Canadian-American who wrote plays, short stories, and novels. His most famous work was *The Happy Time*, which is about the LaFrances, a French-Canadian family living in Ottawa in the 1920s. That novel was later made into a play and movie. Two other novels dealing with the LaFrance family are *My Uncle Louis* and *Hello to Springtime*. Fontaine's writing is usually humorous, and he likes to use surprise endings as he does at the end of the first paragraph in the selection below.

"How My Love Was Sawed in Half" is the story of a young boy who runs away in the summertime to live with a carnival. The title of the story refers to a boy's experiences with the carnival: he fell in love with a girl who worked with a magician, and the magician used to pretend to saw the girl in half.

PRE-READING QUESTIONS

1. Did you ever run away from home? Why? Where did you go?

2. Did you ever want to run away from home? Why?

3. Are you familiar with carnivals? If so, what parts of a carnival do you like? What don't you like? Have you ever seen a person sawed in half at a carnival or a magic show?

4. When you were young, did you ever dream about a "perfect" girl or boy? What were they like?

When I was about twelve, or maybe I was fourteen, I ran away from home one summer. My home was a lovely, cool home. The bees would buzz in our flowerful back yard; great monarch butterflies would arch their way about the phlox and verbena. There would be watermelon on the vine, and red tomatoes. It was all neatly arranged and predictable. That was why I ran away.

My mother and father, very strict parents indeed, thought I had gone to summer camp. My Uncle Louis, a great lover of good wine, thought I had gone to summer camp. All the neighbors thought so, too.

I started for summer camp, but I got off the train because I saw a carnival setting up. I intended to stay only until the next train north. Then I remembered the advice of my uncle: "If you do not see all of this world, you will not be ready for the next."

The carnival was bright as a fairy tale, as noisy and exciting as a hockey game, as colorful as a birthday party.

I roamed about in a daze, smelling the popcorn and candied apples, listening to the singing of the barkers, tasting maple leaves made of sugar, and riding swiftly to the skies in a make-believe airplane.

When the next train had long gone by, and the next after that, I was still wild-eyed and enamored. I was drunk with sound and color. I was in love with movement.

How could my camp, my family, my home, my school, my life vanish so utterly from my heart? What was this magnificence that now took the place of all those small, concrete things that had been my life? It had no name, but it sang and it filled me and made me drunk.

There was nothing I wanted more to do than to stay with the carnival forever. Here, at last, was the place for me. Here was made solid my dream. Life at home, I used to tell myself in the quiet of my small room, was not the way it should be. Life should be vastly more entertaining, more filled with surprises, more provocative of laughter. Here, in the Universal Greater Shows, it was.

*   *   *

I wandered around excitedly. I saw everything. At last I came to Hypo the Hypnotist. His face was painted as if he were not alive, like a strange man—all white, with two red dots at the cheeks.

I watched eagerly as he sawed a woman in half; sawed in half a beautiful girl before my very eyes. I was stunned. Never had I seen this sort of thing, nor had I ever seen a girl so brave and beautiful.

How My Love Was Sawed in Half **97**

She lay there with her head extended from a box, smiling so beautifully and lovingly. She was the girl I had always pictured when I read love stories. She was the girl I had always dreamed about—golden hair, blue eyes, a bright smile, and brave and true.

It did not bother her at all when the saw went through her. She still smiled. And then, miracle! In a few minutes she was restored to perfect wholeness. What lovely magic!

*　　　*　　　*

It came near the time for me to leave. The camp would soon be over, and I had to get home. I had sent letters to my chums to forward to my parents. They were the same letters I always sent from the same camp. But the day came when I was due home. Finally I had to leave this wonderland.

Before I went, I wanted to kiss Belle-Linda and tell her I loved her for her beauty and her bravery. I tried several times to speak to her when she was about to be sawed in half, but Hypo always pushed me away.

*　　　*　　　*

When I got home everything was the same. It was the same cool world, with quiet speech and watermelon on the vine and the giant butterflies in the yard and the August Yellow Transparents now ripe on the tree.

"You did not get very tanned," my mother said.

"I kept out of the sun."

My father said, "Good boy. Too much sun is not good."

Later, my Uncle Louis, full of wine, said, "You have been up to something. You went away with clouds in your eyes, and now there are stars. You must tell me sometime."

In the dead of melancholy winter, I told him one day. He explained to me, "Ah, well, there are two girls, you see. One is the head, and she is folded up, so. The other is the feet, and she is folded up, so. When the man saws, he saws between the two. Understand? It is all a trick."

I smiled and pretended I believed him. He did not understand. He was not, perhaps, in love with anyone at the time.

Glossary

flowerful the writer invented this word to mean full of flowers

arch their way about the phlox and verbena fly among the flowers

indeed intensifies the meaning of *very strict*

summer camp a place were groups of children play in the summer, with supervision

barkers people who call out at carnivals to try to get you to come in and see their show

long gone by passed by a long time ago

Universal Greater Shows the name of the carnival

Belle-Linda the name of the girl who was being sawed in half

August Yellow Transparents the name of a type of apple

up to something busy with something (usually something that is tricky or that is being hidden)

the dead of the middle of

Vocabulary

A. Find the word(s) closest in meaning to the underlined words. Circle the best answer.

1. The flowers and the vegetables were all arranged <u>neatly</u> in the back yard.
   a. together   b. carefully   c. carelessly   d. with a fence

2. When he was at the carnival, the thoughts of his life at home all <u>vanished.</u>
   a. disappeared   b. changed   c. remained   d. appeared

3. He was <u>stunned</u> when Hypo sawed the girl in half.
   a. sad   b. sick   c. happy   d. very surprised

4. After Hypo sawed the girl in half, she was <u>restored</u> to her normal condition.
   a. brought back   b. helped
   c. arranged   d. not able to be in

5. He had a feeling of <u>melancholy</u> when the time came to leave the carnival and go home.
   a. relief   b. anger   c. sadness   d. happiness

B. Complete the sentences with words from the list.

color	sawed	predictable
magic	restored	bright
movement	arranged	exciting

Everything at the carnival seemed ___color___ and ___bright___ to the boy. He was especially attracted to the ___exciting___ and the ___movement___. When the girl was ___restored___ to her normal condition after Hypo ___sawed___ her in half, it seemed like ___magic___ to the boy. It was different from his life at home where everything was ___arranged___ neatly and life was ___predictable___.

Comprehension

1. What was the boy's home like?
2. Why did he run away?
3. Where did he go?
4. Where did everyone think that he went?
5. Why did he like life at the carnival?
6. What did Hypo do?
7. Why did the boy like Belle-Linda?
8. Why did his parents think that he was at camp?
9. What was the trick that Uncle Louis explained to the boy?
10. How did the boy react to Uncle Louis' explanation?
11. What kind of a person was Uncle Louis?

Wordwork

CONNECTING IDEAS

Combine the sentences into one sentence using *who* or *which*. Punctuate carefully.

EXAMPLE

Uncle Louis was a lover of good wine. Uncle Louis thought I had gone to camp.

Uncle Louis, who was a lover of good wine, thought I had gone to camp.

1. My parents were very strict. My parents thought I had gone to summer camp.

   _____

2. My home was lovely and cool. My home was neatly arranged and predictable.

   _____

3. The carnival was bright and noisy. The carnival was attractive to the young boy.

   _____

4. Belle-Linda was brave and beautiful. Belle-Linda lay there with her head extended from a box.

   _____

5. Uncle Louis was happy and drunk. Uncle Louis knew that the boy had been up to something.

   _____

Predictable and Unpredictable

Make a list of actions or situations that would be predictable or unpredictable for you.

Predictable

EXAMPLE

My mother gives me tea when I'm sick.

1. _____
2. _____
3. _____
4. _____
5. _____

Unpredictable

EXAMPLE

I never know when my brother will call me.

1. _____
2. _____
3. _____
4. _____
5. _____

I Thought So, Too

Make up three statements about the story that other students can respond to by saying, "I thought so, too."

EXAMPLE

I thought the boy lived in a nice house.

I thought so, too.

Write the statements here.

1. _____

2. _____

3. _____

Home

1. In the first paragraph, the writer gives some details of the backyard of his home. List some specific details that you remember from a part of your home.

   _____

   _____

2. Choose a month or a season and tell about the weather, the flowers, the fruit, etc. that would be there in your city or town.

   _____

   _____

Never Had I Seen

Write a brief description of something that stunned you. For a dramatic ending, you may begin your last sentence with the phrase "Never had I seen . . ."

_____

_____

_____

———— As ————

The writer writes that the carnival was as bright as a fairy tale, as noisy and exciting as a hockey game, and as colorful as a birthday party.

A. Think of other comparisons you could make and complete the phrases below.

    1. as bright as ———————————————————

    2. as noisy as ————————————————————

    3. as exciting as ——————————————————

    4. as colorful as ——————————————————

B. Now put the phrases into sentences.

    1. ————————————————————————

    2. ————————————————————————

    3. ————————————————————————

    4. ————————————————————————

    5. Write your own: ————————————————

Suggestions for Discussion and Writing ————

1. Young people, and sometimes older people, too, run away from their homes. What are some reasons why people do this?

2. Fontaine writes that his parents were strict. What kinds of attitudes do you think strict parents would have? What would be an ideal relationship between parents and children?

3. How would you write this selection if the events happened in your country? In your composition, answer questions such as: Where would the boy be going for the summer? Where would he run to? How would he travel?

4. Carnivals used to exhibit people such as the "Bearded Lady" and the "Indian Rubber Boy." Why did this happen? Why is it not happening now?

5. The boy had dreamed about an ideal girl. Where do we get our ideas of what a perfect boy/man, or girl/woman would be? Is it a good idea to have dreams like this?

6. Uncle Louis tells his nephew that "if you do not see all of this world, you will not be ready for the next." He is encouraging his nephew to live his life as fully as possible. Do you have any sayings in your culture that reflect this idea?

Independent Study

1. Read another short story by Robert Fontaine. Or, if you can read the original story in the *Atlantic Monthly* (June, 1960), find out what else happened at the carnival.

2. Find out what kinds of shows they have at carnivals.

3. Read about a circus such as the Big Apple Circus or the Ringling Brothers and Barnum and Bailey Circus.

4. Find out who P.T. Barnum and Tom Thumb were.

5. Look up these words and be ready to describe the differences in meaning: *neat, methodical, tidy, orderly, shipshape, systematic.*

6. Look up these words and be ready to describe the differences in meaning: *drunk, intoxicated, tipsy, blotto.* Are there any other words you know to describe this condition?

2

Estelle

Darryl Ponicsan

Darryl Ponicsan (b. 1938) is an American author who lives in California. He has a Master of Arts degree from Cornell University and has taught in various American schools. He has written eight novels, one of which, *Cinderella Liberty*, was made into a motion picture. Two of his screenplays are *Taps* (1981) and *Vision Quest* (1984).

"Estelle" is taken from *Andoshen, Pa.*, a novel which describes life in a small poor mining town in rural Pennsylvania. The town was not a beautiful place. The author quotes from a letter about the town which he received from his parents. They said ". . . at least if there's a war they won't bomb us. The planes will look down and think we've already been bombed." In this selection we read about Estelle Wowak, a young girl who graduates from high school and goes to work in a department store. She dreams of the time when she can leave her useless job and go to New York. Finally, she does it.

PRE-READING QUESTIONS

1. Do you know anyone who is bored with their job? Why are they bored?

2. Do you know anyone who has left a small city or town to go to a big city? What happened?

3. What do you think makes a job interesting?

4. What city do you think would be the most exciting?

Estelle Wowak graduated from Andoshen High School without any particular honors or skills.

She went to work as a counter girl at Newberry's Five and Dime, first at the candy counter, then at notions, by her own request because she was getting fat from eating the few pieces always left in her hand after weighing a pound on the scale for a customer.

It made her mother sad to see Estelle begin her working life at the five and dime store in a town that could hold only the worst of its young men, the dreamers, the rowdies, the pool shooters, boys destined for nothing but varying degrees of self-deception. The other boys were gone to colleges and jobs in the cities, to return only on weekends with their suitcases full of dirty clothes for their mothers to wash. They were eager to date those local girls who had remained at home, to impress them with their new ways and knowledge, and to take them parking in the cemeteries as though it were their right. Even with her own daughter this could happen, until when she did marry, she would have to marry a hard man, an old man, a drinking man, any man.

Her anxiety was Estelle's as well, especially after two years had passed and she was still behind the notions counter. To think of it made her blood ripple. The girls in the present graduating class were two *years* behind her. In high school, she had hardly known them, and now they were out and off to adventures, while she spent her days imagining breaking in a new girl to take over her job.

Estelle ran the scene over and over again in her imagination because some day soon she was actually going to break in a new girl. She was going to go to New York. She was going to get a room right in the city and find a job as a secretary, and if she couldn't find one, she would go to the five and dime, there must be fifty of them in New York, and with her experience she would have no trouble getting a job. Working in the five and dime in New York is not like working in the five and dime in Andoshen. There you're really dealing with the public. You probably never see the same customer twice.

She would get a room in the middle of the city, and every night she would walk down Broadway and once a week she would go to Radio City Music Hall, on Saturday, and to the zoo on Sunday. After a while she would be like any other city person, and strangers would stop her on the street and ask for directions to the Statue of

Liberty. She would tell them (because she would know) in a clipped, familiar way, and measure the distance in minutes instead of miles, like a city person.

This is what she was planning on, this is what she prepared for when she repeatedly broke in the imaginary new girl.

This is what happened:

She quit on a Monday, at closing time, explaining to the manager, "I'm sorry, I can't put it off any longer. I've got to get going to New York before I have even one more day to think about it."

"It happens like that. You should get it out of your system."

"I feel bad about not breaking in a new girl for you."

"Oh, don't worry, we can take care of that."

Estelle knew that it would take all of ten minutes for him to break in a new girl. I have wasted two years of my life, she thought.

"Would you like me to give your pay to your mother, or shall I mail it to you?"

Estelle looked at the notions counter and saw herself gone from it.

"Do you have all your stuff with you?"

Over her arm she carried her smock, the name pin still attached.

The manager looked at his watch. "Then I guess I'll wish you good luck."

He shook her hand, took a "Girl Wanted" sign from the file cabinet, and walked her to the front door. He propped the sign against the window, locked the door behind them, and said, "Bye."

The next morning she boarded a Trailways to New York City, and the driver assured her that the bus stopped right in the middle of the city.

She disembarked at Port Authority, her heart full of adventure, but on the street she clutched her bags and looked around, frightened. Where was Ella's Lunch? Where was the Capital Theater? Wadden Park? The brewery? Where was the five and dime? Where was Kayo Mackey and his pool sheets? Where was Duncan from the Majestic?

A man approached her on the street in front of Port Authority. His clothes were dirty and he smelled.

"Can I get you a cab? Where are you staying? I'll carry your bags for you."

Her breath was caught in her throat. She forced it out and said, "No, thank you, no, thank you. I'm waiting for someone. My husband's picking me up here."

The man went away.

She stood on the sidewalk at the station, clutching her bags, feeling the force of the city against her body, the air in her nostrils, the noise against her ears like the hammers of hell, the tall buildings pressing down on her head. She stood there in the New York City summer for fifteen minutes, until her clothes were wet with perspiration and her panties clung to the fold of her body.

She turned around, went back into Port Authority and waited six hours at the boarding gate for the next bus to Andoshen.

Her job at Newberry's had been filled by a young widow named Donna.

The following day a cigar roller died at the Savannah Hand-Made Cigars factory and she got that vacant job.

Glossary

notions   variety of small things for sale

five and dime   a store like Woolworth's that sells inexpensive things

pool   a game (billiards)

take . . . parking   engage in sexual activities in a car

ran the scene over   imagined the scene a lot

break in (a person)   train; teach a job to someone

a clipped, familiar way   Estelle thinks that people in New York shorten their words and talk quickly and informally

put off   postpone

get it out of your system   do something that has been bothering you for some time so that you won't have the problem anymore

Vocabulary _____

A. Find the word(s) closest in meaning to the underlined word(s). Circle the best answer.

1. Estelle's <u>anxiety</u> came from her feeling that her job in the department store was a useless job.
   a. tiredness   b. excitement   c. worry   d. sadness

2. Before she left for New York, she was going to <u>break in</u> a new girl.
   a. find   b. pay   c. train   d. steal

3. While she was planning to leave, Estelle often thought about the <u>imaginary</u> new girl who would take her job.
   a. clever   b. not real   c. imaginative   d. actual

4. She <u>quit</u> her job on a Monday.
   a. left   b. found   c. applied for   d. changed

5. When she was in New York, she made sure that she <u>clutched</u> her bag.
   a. held tightly   b. sent   c. tied   d. filled

B. Complete the sentences with the words from the list.

skills	impress	eager	repeatedly
self-deception	deal with	imaginary	hardly
adventure	put off	bored	
imagination			

Estelle didn't need many _____ for her job at the notions counter, but she was _____. She was _____ to leave. In her _____, she saw herself in New York. New York was going to be a wonderful _____. There she would _____ a variety of customers and _____ strangers with her knowledge of the city. She _____ imagined her life in New York and decided not to _____ her trip any longer. But her wonderful life in New York was only _____. When she went there, it _____ satisfied her. Her dream was a

_____.

Comprehension _____

1. Where did Estelle work?
2. Why was Estelle's mother unhappy?
3. Why was Estelle anxious?
4. What kinds of jobs did Estelle expect to get in New York?
5. For Estelle, what was going to be the difference between working in Andoshen and in New York?
6. What would Estelle do for recreation in New York?
7. What does Estelle mean when she says she would "measure the distance in minutes instead of miles?"
8. What was the manager's reaction when Estelle said that she was quitting her job?
9. Why was Estelle unhappy in New York?
10. What happened when Estelle went back to Andoshen?
11. Do you think Estelle will be happy in Andoshen? Why or why not?

Wordwork _____

CONNECTING IDEAS

Combine the sentences into one sentence. You may have to change some nouns to pronouns and you may want to omit some words. Study the example.

EXAMPLE

Uncle Louis liked good wine. Uncle Louis enjoyed good food. Uncle Louis loved all the ladies.

_____*Uncle Louis liked good wine, enjoyed good food,*_____

_____*and loved all the ladies.*_____

1. The manager shook her hand. The manager took a Girl Wanted sign from the cabinet. The manager walked Estelle to the front door.

   _____

   _____

2. The manager put a sign in the window. The manager locked the door behind them. The manager said, "Bye."

   _____

   _____

3. Estelle was going to go to New York. Estelle was going to get a room in the city. Estelle was going to find a job as a secretary.

   _____

   _____

4. She would walk down Broadway. She would go to Radio City Music Hall. She would visit the zoo.

   _____

   _____

5. Estelle turned around. She went back into the Port Authority. She waited six hours for the next bus.

   _____

   _____

What If . . .

Imagine that the story was different. Tell **what** might have happened
if. . . .

1. Estelle's cousin went to New York with her.

_____

_____

_____

_____

_____

2. Estelle arrived in New York at the airport.

_____

_____

_____

_____

_____

3. Estelle ran away to the capital of your country.

_____

_____

_____

_____

_____

Things I've Always Wanted to Do

1. Write down three things that you have always wanted to do. For each thing, tell why you haven't been able to do it yet.

   _____   _____   _____

   a. _____
      _____
      _____

   b. _____
      _____
      _____

   c. _____
      _____
      _____

2. If you could live in any city in the world, where would you go and what would you do there? Write about it.

   _____
   _____
   _____
   _____
   _____

City and Town

1. People who live in big cities often dream of living in small towns or in the country. People who live in small towns or in the country often dream of living in big cities. List some of the good and bad points of living in big cities or in small towns/country.

Cities

Good	Bad
_____	_____
_____	_____
_____	_____
_____	_____
_____	_____

Towns/County

Good	Bad
_____	_____
_____	_____
_____	_____
_____	_____
_____	_____

2. The writer feels that city people measure distance in minutes, not in miles. What are some other specific differences between life in a big city and life in a small town.

_____

_____

_____

Loneliness

1. What are some of the things you can do so that you won't become lonely in a big city? In a small town?

_____

_____

_____

2. What is the difference between being lonely and being alone? Can you be lonely in a crowd?

_____

_____

_____

Coming Home

When people come back from living in another place, their attitude towards their home and the people in their hometown often changes. The attitudes of the hometown people towards those who have been away may also change. If this has happened to you or to someone you know, describe the experience.

_____

_____

_____

Dialogues

1. Make up a brief conversation between Estelle and a customer at the candy counter in Andoshen.

   Estelle: _____

   Customer: _____

   Estelle: _____

   Customer: _____

2. Make up a brief conversation between Estelle and a stranger who asks her for directions in New York.

   Estelle: _____

   Stranger: _____

   Estelle: _____

   Stranger: _____

Suggestions for Discussion and Writing

1. Describe the first job you ever had. Tell if it was interesting, boring, easy, hard, busy, etc. Be specific.

2. Sometimes people are disappointed when they finally do the things that they have always wanted to. If you or anyone you know has had an experience like that, describe it.

3. When you were reading the story, did you think that Estelle was going to be successful in New York? If you thought she wasn't going to be successful, at what point in the story did you think so? Why?

4. A recent visitor to Paris, who came from a rural area, said: "There are too many ads everywhere, there are too many buildings, there is too much noise. The men spend too much on drink, and the women spend too much on clothes." What do you think of his reaction?

5. The author writes that the college boys came home to impress the girls of Andoshen with their new ways and knowledge. What kinds of things do you think would impress the girls? What impresses you? Why do we want to impress other people?

Independent Study

1. Read another chapter in the book *Andoshen, Pa.* or in another of Ponicsan's novels. Are the people that you read about happy?

2. Look up these words and be prepared to describe the differences in meaning: *date, engagement, going steady, blind date, affair, flirt, sweetheart.*

3. Check the meaning of these terms: *friend, acquaintance, girl/boy friend, fiancé/fiancée, significant other.* What other English words describe male-female relationships?

4. Find a song whose words could be used to talk about what happened to Estelle. (For example, there is a Brazilian song whose title is "Go Back Home.")

5. The American author John Steinbeck also wrote about poor struggling working men and women. Read a selection from *Cannery Row* or *Tortilla Flat* or from another of Steinbeck's novels.

3

Jones Beach

Nicholas Gagarin

Nicholas Gagarin (b. 1948) grew up in Connecticut and attended Harvard College, where he wrote for the campus newspaper. The following selection was taken from Gagarin's novel *Windsong*, a story of young people and the way they experienced life during the 1960s. "Jones Beach," which is the title of a chapter in the novel, is a public beach on Long Island, New York.

In the reading below, the author describes the wonderful feeling of freedom he has when he starts to drive to the beach one morning in June.

PRE-READING QUESTIONS

1. What does it mean to "feel free?" When do you feel free?

2. What do you do when you get tired of doing things that you have to do every day?

3. How do you like to spend your vacations?

Connecticut is beautiful in early June. The rolling hills are green and beckoning, the leaves on the trees full and deep. The land is fertile, washed and nourished by the spring rains; and in the rich soil of gardens, peas and carrots are appearing. The mornings are warm and clear, the sun rising early so that by midday you can get a taste of the summer heat that will follow in July and August.

On a day like this, on a Wednesday morning in early June, it is possible to feel free; for school is over for the year and the summer lies ahead. And so, on this Wednesday morning, you get up early in the morning and go out for a drive in your car, because you like that, it's fun. You drive along a little country road, the top of your car down, and you feel the chill of the early morning air, as the wind blows all around you. You feel the chill in your neck and behind your ears, but the sun is getting higher in the sky; it will be warmer soon. You feel your hair being blown in a thousand directions, and that's fine. It's good to feel the long brown hair blowing around your ears, it's good sometimes to look down onto the road next to your car and see the shadow of the car, with you inside, and your hair blowing in the wind. You drive through patches of sunlight and shade; the air is dry, so you feel the difference. And you feel free, being free.

It is hard to be free. It is probably one of the hardest things in the world, because the world doesn't leave much room for freedom. There isn't much space given you, there aren't many people around you who are free. Everyone has miles to go and things to do, and the world catches you up, it carries you along, it doesn't give you much room. But it's also so easy to be free. Being free is probably one of the easiest things in the world, too, only almost nobody realizes it. Because we are free: we were born free, we live free, and we will die free. Only we don't realize it. There is always so much going on, perhaps, always so much to do, that we never stop and look at what's happening. Until some day, some Wednesday morning in early June, when you get up in the morning when it's still chilly and you go for a drive in your car, along a country road, through little towns, past little homes and farmhouses, and suddenly you realize it, you know it: you are free, free always, free forever.

That is all it takes. You like to drive, you like driving your little sports car with the top down, and that's all it takes. And you find yourself getting high, as high as the sky, because it is wonderful to be there, in that time and in that place, and you would exchange it for none other. You get stoned just by driving, and you begin to think that maybe they're all wrong, maybe all the ones who have taught you are wrong. Because they've taught you that what goes up always comes down. That's physics, after all, that's science and knowledge, and when an apple falls from a tree, it's going to hit someone who's sitting beneath. That's the way things are. But you begin to wonder. Maybe things don't have to be that way. Maybe it's possible to go up and never come down, to stay up, to be always up, to be always stoned.

Maybe there is a place there, a place that the birds know, a place which men have reached for. Maybe it really does exist, and if you could find it you would never leave, you would never need to leave or want to leave, because the place is perfect and you are perfectly stoned. So you drive along, out driving just for the fun of driving, and then maybe you say to yourself, "The hell with that place, things are fine here. I like it here." For you feel good, there, feel good driving along, and you think you could probably feel good any place doing anything. The hell with the birds, let them have their place, because you've got yours, and you like it fine. The hell with wondering and worrying. School's out, it was out five days ago, you've passed your exams, so you don't need to worry again for three months. It's the summer now, the beginning of the summer. It's a beautiful day, and you don't need anything more. Except maybe a little music, so you turn on the radio. It's warmer now, it's just right, and the air that flows over these hills, past these homes and farmhouses, and down these country roads, the air is fresh and clean.

Glossary

for   because

the top of your car down   this refers to a convertible car whose top can be folded back

the world catches you up   becoming involved in many activities

getting high   feeling as if you were drunk or affected by drugs

be stoned; get stoned   affected by drugs

school's out   the school year is finished

Vocabulary

A. Find the word(s) closest in meaning to the underlined word. Circle the best answer.

1. On a beautiful day it seems that nature is <u>beckoning</u> you to go outside.
   a. warning   b. calling   c. forcing   d. tricking

2. Even in the summertime you may feel a <u>chill</u> early in the morning.
   a. warmth   b. raindrop   c. coldness   d. wind

3. It was a cloudy day, but there were <u>patches</u> of light on the highway.
   a. small areas   b. large areas
   c. explosions   d. movements

4. The spring rains <u>nourished</u> the land.
   a. flooded   b. dried   c. fed   d. chilled

B. Complete the sentences with the words from the list.

sunlight	free	drive
freedom	fun	feel
wind	warm	realize
	clear	blow

Many people like to _____. They feel _____ as

they look ahead on the road and see the _____. They

_____ free as the _____ starts to _____ on

their faces. They know that it is _____ to drive on a

_____ and _____ day, but many do not _____

that their pleasure comes from a feeling of _____.

Comprehension

1. When does the story take place?
2. Why does the writer feel free?
3. Where does he go?
4. What does he like about driving?
5. Does he think it is easy or hard for us to be free?
6. According to the writer, why don't we realize that we can be free?
7. What does the writer think about the idea that "That's the way things are"? (Paragraph 4)
8. What makes the writer feel good?

Wordwork

CONNECTING IDEAS

Combine the sentences into one sentence using the word *so*. Punctuate carefully. Study the example.

EXAMPLE

The sun rises early. By midday you can feel the summer heat.

The sun rises early, so by midday you can feel the summer heat.

1. You want to feel the wind blowing all around you. You put the top of your car down.

2. School is over for the year. You don't have to wake up early.

3. The air is dry. You can feel the difference between sunlight and shade.

4. Everyone has things to do. They don't have time to be free.

5. There might be a perfect place somewhere in the world. You would never want to leave it.

_____

6. He turned on the radio. He could hear the weather report.

_____

7. I needed to be by myself. I went for a drive.

_____

8. They passed their exams. They don't have to study for three months.

_____

Seasons

1. List the seasons in your country.

_____

2. For each season, write one or two sentences that describe that season.

_____

_____

_____

_____

3. Which season do you like best and why?

_____

4. Which season do you like least and why?

_____

Vacations

1. How much vacation time do people usually have in your country?

_____

2. Where do families like to go for vacation?

_____

3. Where do single people like to go for vacation?

   _____

4. Where do newly married couples like to go for vacation?

   _____

5. Where did you go on your last vacation? Why?

How Would You Feel?

Complete the following sentences by describing how you *would feel*.
Study the example:

EXAMPLE

   If I were riding in a convertible car,

   _____ *I would feel the wind in my hair.* _____

1. If I were walking in the rain, I would _____

2. If I were flying in a small plane, _____

3. If I were walking alone in a city late at night, _____

4. If I ate too much, _____

5. If I rode on a roller coaster, _____

6. If I were watching a horror movie, _____

7. If I were riding down a steep hill on a motorcycle, _____

   _____

8. Make up your own sentence. _____

   _____

What Goes Up Always Comes Down

1. What does Gagarin say about the idea expressed in the sentence "What goes up always comes down?" (Paragraph 4)

   _____

   _____

   _____

2. Describe something that you were taught that you later found out was not true.

   _____

   _____

   _____

Miles To Go

Gagarin uses the phrase "miles to go" in his novel. This phrase comes from a poem by Robert Frost. Here is one stanza of that poem:

> The woods are lovely, dark and deep,
> But I have promises to keep,
> And miles to go before I sleep,
> And miles to go before I sleep.

1. What do you think Frost is saying in this stanza?

   _____

   _____

   _____

2. Copy the sentence from the story in which Gagarin uses the phrases "miles to go."

   _____

   _____

3. What is Gagarin's point. Is it similar to Frost's?

_____

_____

_____

Suggestions for Discussion and Writing _____

1. What do you think of Gagarin's ideas? Can we be as free as he suggests? Why or why not?
2. Describe one vacation that you especially enjoyed. Where did you go and what did you do?
3. Can you think of a time in your life when you felt really free?
4. Does Gagarin's definition of freedom apply only to young people?
5. During the 1960's, smoking marijuana and taking mind-altering drugs were more acceptable than they are now. What happened to change the public's attitude toward drugs?
6. Jones Beach is a favorite place for families as well as for teenagers. Why do you think teenagers like to go to beaches?

Independent Study _____

1. Find the complete poem "Stopping by Woods on a Snowy Evening" by Robert Frost and write a brief description of the ideas in the poem.
2. Gagarin is now in his mid-40s. Imagine that he has a family. Do you think he would have the same ideas? Why or why not? If he did have the same ideas, how do you think he would spend his day?
3. Who was Jack Kerouac? Read a selection from his book *On the Road*.
4. Look up the definition of the word *freedom*. Why is it difficult to define a word like that?
5. Go to the library and read an article about college students in the 1960s. How were they different from college students in the 1990s?

Review

1. Compare the boy in "How My Love Was Sawed in Half" with Estelle. They both wanted to go someplace to accomplish something. What did they want? How did they try to do it? How successful were they?

2. What advice do you think the young man in "Jones Beach" would give Estelle? What advice do you think the boy in "How My Love Was Sawed in Half" would give Estelle?

3. Which characters in these three stories would probably agree most with each other? Why?

4. What do you think each of the characters will be doing ten years after the times of the stories?

5. What would have happened if the boy had gone to New York City? What would have happened if the college student had driven to New York City?

6. Which character do you think you are most similar to?

7. Imagine that the college student had met Estelle at Jones Beach. What kind of conversation would have taken place? Imagine that the college student had met Estelle at the candy counter in Andoshen. What kind of conversation would have taken place?

8. Look up the song "Over the Rainbow" from the movie *The Wizard of Oz*. How are the ideas expressed in this song related to the stories in this unit?

UNIT FIVE
Values: What is Important?

UNIT INTRODUCTION

Fiction often shows us what is important in life. We are usually very busy with the details of everyday life, and we do not appreciate the important moments of our lives. In "Leaf" and "Loaf," William Saroyan writes of the simple things that most of us can see and feel and taste. In Arturo Vivante's story "A Game of Light and Shade," we read of a blind man who cannot enjoy the sights of this world, but he still finds beauty in life. And Russell Banks, in "My Mother's Memoirs," calls our attention to the importance of love and to our need for relationships.

UNIT PRE-READING

1. If you had nothing to do tomorrow, what would you do?

2. What things in the world around you give you the greatest pleasures?

3. Many writers have said that life is short but art is long. What do you think they mean?

Leaf and Loaf

William Saroyan

William Saroyan (1908–1981) was an American writer of Armenian background who wrote short stories, plays, and novels. He wrote mostly about the very different ways in which ordinary people enjoy daily life in the United States. *The Daring Young Man on the Flying Trapeze,* his first collection of stories, is probably one of his best-known works. In 1939, Saroyan won the Pulitzer Prize for his play *The Time of Your Life,* but he would not accept it because he said he did not believe in literary prizes.

These selections are taken from the book *Papa, You're Crazy.* In that book, Saroyan describes a boy and his father who go to different places in San Francisco and enjoy the experiences of everyday life.

PRE-READING QUESTIONS

1. What is one object that you think is very beautiful? What makes it beautiful?

2. When you have free time, how do you like to spend it?

3. What did your mother or father teach you was important in life?

4. When you think about getting a job, what values are most important?

LEAF

At last we went out and stood on the lawn and watched the sun go down, and my father said, "If it weren't for art, we'd have vanished from the face of the earth long ago."

What art *really* is, though, and what a human being really is, and what the world really is. I just don't *know*, that's all.

Standing there, watching the sun go down into the sea, my father said, "In every house there ought to be an art table on which, one by one, things are placed, so that everybody in that house might look at the things very carefully, and *see* them."

"What would *you* put on a table like that?"

"A leaf. A coin. A button. A stone. A small piece of torn newspaper. An apple. An egg. A pebble. A flower. A dead insect. A shoe."

"Everybody's *seen* those things."

"Of course. But nobody *looks* at them, and that's what art is. To look at familiar things as if they had never before been seen. A plain sheet of paper with typing on it. A necktie. A pocketknife. A key. A fork. A cup. A bottle. A bowl. A walnut."

"What about a baseball? A baseball's a beautiful thing."

"It certainly is. You would place something on the table and look at it. The next morning you would take it away, and put something else there—*anything*, for there is nothing made by nature or by man that doesn't deserve to be looked at particularly."

Now, the sun was gone all the way into the sea. There was a lot of orange light on the water, and in the sky above the water. Legion of Honor Hill grew dark, and my father brought out a cigarette and lighted it and inhaled and then let the smoke out of his nose and mouth, and he said, "Well, boy, there's another day of the wonderful world gone forever."

"*New* day tomorrow, though."

"What do you say we drive to the Embarcadero and look at the ships from all over the world?"

*   *   *

LOAF

We loafed through the whole town, because that was what we had planned to do. It was nothing more than just another little town with another bunch of people living in it. We saw some of the people. All of a sudden I noticed their eyes.

This made me laugh.

"Tell me about it," my father said.

"Eyes," I said. "We sure have got *eyes*, haven't we?"

"Very good," my father said.

He began to sing, *"I saw your eyes, your wonderful eyes."*

Pretty soon he stopped singing and began to breathe deeply.

"Somebody's baking bread somewhere. Would you like some fresh bread?"

"I sure would."

We walked to the corner, then *around* the corner, but we didn't find a bakery there, so we went back to where we had been, and near there we found the place, but the door was locked.

My father knocked, and then we saw a man in a baker's white coat with flour on his hands and face come to the door and open it.

"We open at seven," the man said. "It's not six yet."

"What are you baking back there?"

"Bread and rolls."

"How about letting me buy some? I don't often get a change to eat freshly baked bread."

"You want to come in, then?" the baker said, so my father and I went in. We followed the man to where he and his wife were baking bread. It was clean and warm back there. The metal racks had new loaves on them and new rolls.

"Help yourself," the baker said.

My father took a loaf of French bread from among half a dozen the baker's wife brought out of the oven on a long wooden spade and held out to him, and then she brought him a lot of rolls on the spade. My father took half a dozen rolls, too. He gave me one, and he took a bite out of another. The big loaf he put in his coat pocket just the way it was.

"Sit down," the baker said. "There's some cheese over there on that little table. Help yourself."

My father and I went to the little table where the baker and his wife sat and ate bread and cheese, and we sat there.

"Do you know the baker?"

"Never saw him before in my life."

The baker came over and broke open a roll and put some cheese in it. I thought he was going to bite into it himself, but he handed the roll to me and said, "Always remember bread and cheese. When everything else looks bad, remember bread and cheese, and you'll be all right."

"Yes, sir."

"That's why I'm a baker," he said. "I tried a lot of other things, but this is the work for me."

Glossary

at last   finally

what do you say we drive   let's drive

help yourself   take what you want

Vocabulary

A. Find the word(s) closest in meaning to the underlined word. Circle the best answer.

1. He never expected to find an <u>insect</u> inside his watch.
   a. small stone   b. coin   c. bug   d. leaf

2. She couldn't walk very well because of the <u>pebble</u> in her shoe.
   a. small stone   b. small hole   c. gum   d. sock

3. When they were walking past the roses, they decided to stop and <u>inhale.</u>
   a. touch   b. breathe out   c. look   d. breathe in

4. Not many people decide to spend a whole day <u>loafing.</u>
   a. baking bread   b. doing nothing
   c. exercising   d. eating

5. There was a <u>bunch</u> of people in the center of the town.
   a. group   b. couple   c. movement   d. rebellion

B. Complete the sentences with words from the list. There may be more than one good choice for each blank. A few words must be used more than once.

watch	beautiful	art
see	wonderful	
familiar		

A tree is certainly a _____ object, but not many people would call it an object of _____. While people pay to _____ a sports event, very few would pay to _____ a tree. But if you look at a _____ tree in the springtime, you will _____ many things you haven't seen before. You may decide that a tree is a _____ thing.

to	near	in
at	with	on
of	for	from
		through

The boy was _____ his father, and the two of them walked _____ the town looking _____ the people. When the father smelled fresh bread, they walked _____ a bakery that was _____ them. The baker said that the bakery opened _____ seven, but he let them come in. The father took a loaf _____ French bread _____ the baker's wife and put it _____ his pocket. Then the baker took a roll and put some cheese _____ it. The baker liked his job. He said, "This is the work _____ me."

Comprehension – Leaf _____

1. Where were the boy and his father standing when the selection begins?
2. The father says that there should be something in every house. What?
3. Why did the father think that every house should have an art table?
4. What are some things that the father would put on the table?
5. What would the boy put on the table?
6. Why was there orange light on the water?
7. What is the father's attitude toward life?

Comprehension — Loaf

1. Why were the boy and his father loafing?
2. How did the father know that there was a bakery near them?
3. What time did the bakery usually open?
4. What were the baker and his wife baking?
5. Did the father know the baker?
6. What did the baker say that expressed his attitude toward life?

Wordwork

CONNECTING IDEAS

The following sentences are not in the best order. Rearrange the sentences, in an order that shows how the ideas are connected. Write the paragraph below. You can combine sentences and add connectives if you wish.

1. We watched the sun. Another day was gone. The sun went down. We stood on the lawn. The sky was full of orange light. We went outside. The place grew dark.

_____

_____

_____

_____

_____

_____

_____

2. The father asked him if they could come in. The bakery was near them. The baker's wife gave them bread and rolls. They found a bakery. The father knocked on the door. The baker invited them in. The baker said the bakery wasn't open yet.

_____

_____

_____

_____

_____

_____

_____

_____

3. Combine the sentences into one sentence. You may have to change nouns to pronouns, and you may have to change the order of the sentences. Use connectives to combine the sentences.

   a. My father lighted a cigarette. We stood on the lawn. We watched the sun go down.

   _____

   _____

   b. I don't know what art is. I don't know what a human being is. I don't know what the world is.

   _____

   _____

   c. My father was standing there. My father was watching the sun go down. My father said, "Every house should have an art table."

   _____

   _____

d. My father took out a cigarette. My father inhaled the smoke. My father let the smoke out of his nose and mouth.

_____

e. Every house should have an art table. Everybody could look at things carefully. Everybody could really see things.

_____

f. My father said something. "Everybody's seen familiar things." Nobody looks at those things.

_____

_____

Look at and See, Listen to and Hear

During a day we see many things, but often we do not look at them carefully. Similarly we hear things but often do not listen to them. Look at something that you see every day and describe it carefully. Then listen to something you hear every day and describe it.

1. Every day I see _____. When I look at it carefully, I notice

_____

2. Every day I see _____. When I look at them carefully, I notice

_____

3. Every day I hear _____. When I listen to it carefully, I

_____

4. Every day I hear _____. When I listen to them carefully, I

_____

Familiar and Unfamiliar Things

1. What are some familiar things that you do not have with you now? They may be things that were in your home or your country or things that existed in your childhood.

2. What are some familiar sounds that you do not hear now?

3. What are some unfamiliar things that you have seen recently?

4. What are some unfamiliar sounds that you have heard recently?

5. Choose a familiar object and bring it to class, but do not show it to anyone. Describe it to the class and see if anyone can guess what it is from your description.

Art

1. The father of the narrator says that there ought to be an art table in every home. What would you put on such a table?

2. The father believes that art is a way of giving special attention to the familiar things of life.
   a. Describe a painting that you know which illustrates this idea of art.
   b. Describe a story or a poem that you know which illustrates this idea of art.
   c. Do you agree with the father's idea? Do you know any paintings or writings that illustrate a different idea of art?

Parents and Children

The boy and his father seem to spend a lot of time together.

1. What are some things that parents usually do together with their children in your culture?

   _____

   _____

2. What was a favorite thing that you remember doing with one of your parents? Compare your answer to that of other students.

   _____

   _____

Smells

One of the most delicious smells is that of fresh bread. List some other things that you think smell very good. Try to describe the smell.

   _____

   _____

   _____

   _____

Combinations

The baker thinks that bread and cheese is a wonderful combination. What do you think combines well with the things in the list below?

1. music and _____

2. ice cream and _____

3. a sunset and _____

4. a vacation and _____

5. a boy and _____

Write three of your favorite combinations.

1. _____ and _____

2. _____ and _____

3. _____ and _____

Suggestions for Discussion and Writing _____

1. Describe a particular day when you and a parent or a relative had a good time together.

2. The father thinks that the world is wonderful. Describe someone you know who has a similar attitude.

3. Describe someone you know who has an attitude which is very different from the father's.

4. What do you think the father meant when he said, "If it weren't for art, we'd have vanished from the face of the earth long ago."

5. What do you think the baker meant when he said, ". . . remember bread and cheese, and you'll be all right."?

6. What do you think Saroyan was trying to show us in these stories?

Independent Study

1. Read another short story by Saroyan and be ready to tell it to the class.

2. Look up these words and be prepared to describe the differences in meaning: *stone, rock, pebble, boulder.*

3. Look up these words and be prepared to describe the differences in meaning: *glass, tumbler, goblet, mug, cup.*

4. Read the story "A Small Good Thing," in Raymond Carver's book *Cathedral.* Compare the baker in that story to the baker in "Loaf." In what ways are they similar?

5. The title "Loaf" has two very different meanings for the story. What are the two meanings? Find five other English words that have two quite different meanings.

6. Look up the definition of art in several dictionaries. Then write your own definition.

7. Exploring a new city is exciting. Describe a city or town that you have explored.

2

A Game of Light and Shade

Arturo Vivante

Arturo Vivante (b. 1923) was born in Italy where he earned his medical degree and practiced medicine until he moved to the United States in the 1950s. He now practices writing full time. He has written novels and short stories, and many of his stories have been published in *The New Yorker* magazine. His latest short story collection is called *The Tales of Arturo Vivante* (1990).

In the following selection, which was taken from *Run to the Waterfall*, Vivante creates a story about a blind man who climbs the three-hundred foot tower of the town hall of Siena, a city in Italy.

PRE-READING QUESTIONS

1. What physical pleasures do you think blind people get from the world around them?

2. Have you ever been hurt so that you couldn't use a part of your body? If so, how did you feel? What couldn't you do?

3. Do you have any friends who have physical disabilities? How do they overcome them?

It was a sunny winter day. I had gone up and down the tower, and felt pleased with myself for having taken this initiative, when, outside the little door at the foot, a blind man came toward me. He was a pale, thin man, with sparse black hair and dark glasses that gave him an impenetrable look. He kept close to the inner wall of the courtyard, grazing it with his arm. On reaching the door, he touched the jamb and sharply turned inside. In a moment, he disappeared up the staircase. I stood still, looking at the empty space left by the open door, and at the little plaque that said "To the Tower" nailed to the wall. I felt compelled to follow.

I didn't follow closely. I caught up with him in the ticket office. There I was surprised to see the attendant selling him a ticket as though he were any other visitor. The man fumbled for it, sweeping a little space of desk with his hand until he had it, but the attendant didn't seem to take any notice. Then, with the ticket in one hand and touching the wall with the fingers of the other, he reached the staircase leading to the terrace.

I stood by the desk, watching him until he was out of earshot. "That man is blind," I said to the attendant, and expected him to show some concern, but he just looked at me with his sleepy eyes. He was a heavy man who seemed all one piece with his chair and desk. "He's blind," I repeated.

He looked at me vacantly.

"What would a blind man want to climb up the tower for?" I asked.

He didn't answer.

"Not the view certainly," I said. "Perhaps he wants to jump."

His mouth opened a little. Should he do something? The weight of things was against him. He didn't stir. "Well, let's hope not," he said, and looked down at a crossword puzzle he had begun.

The blind man was now out of sight. I turned toward the staircase.

"The ticket," the attendant said, rising from his chair. It seemed the only thing that could move him.

I handed him a fifty-lira piece, and he detached a ticket from his book. Then I hurried up the staircase.

The man hadn't gone as far as I imagined. Much less time had passed than I thought. A third of the way up the tower, I heard his step. I slowed down and followed him at a little distance. He went up slowly, and stopped from time to time. When he got to the terrace, I was a dozen steps behind. But as I reached it, he wasn't to be seen. I dashed to the first corner of the bell tower, around the next, and saw him.

At last, after ten minutes, I approached him. "Excuse me," I said with the greatest courtesy I could summon, "but I am very curious to know why you came up."

"You'd never guess," he said.

"Not the view, I take it, or the fresh air on this winter day."

"No," he said, and he assumed the amused expression of one who poses a puzzle.

"Tell me," I said.

He smiled. "Perhaps, coming up the stairs, you will have noticed—and yet, not being blind, perhaps you won't—how not just light but sun pours into the tower through the narrow, slitlike windows here and there, so that one can feel the change—the cool staircase suddenly becomes quite warm, even in winter—and how up here behind the merlons there is shade, but as soon as one goes opposite a crenel one finds the sun. In all of Siena there is no place so good as this for feeling the contrast between light and shade. It isn't the first time that I've come up."

He stepped into the shade. "I am in the shade," he said. "There is a merlon there." He moved into the sunlight. "Now I am opposite a crenel," he said. We went down the bell tower. "An arch is there," he said.

"You never miss. And the sun isn't even very strong," I said.

"Strong enough," he said, and added, "Now I'm behind a bell."

Coming back down onto the terrace, he went around it. "Light, shade, light, shade," he said, and seemed as pleased as a child who, in a game of hopscotch, jumps from square to square.

We went down the tower together. "A window there," he said, up near the top. "Another window," he said, when we were halfway down.

I left him, gladdened as one can only be by the sunlight.

Glossary

at the foot   at the bottom (of the tower)

jamb   side of a doorway

caught up with   reached, came to

earshot   hearing distance

I take it   I believe, I assume

merlon   the solid part of a wall between crenels

crenel   a space in a wall

Vocabulary _____

A. Find the word(s) closest in meaning to the underlined word. Circle the best answer.

1. The blind man had sparse black hair.
   a. thick   b. dark   c. thin   d. straight

2. The writer felt compelled to follow the blind man up the staircase.
   a. hesitant   b. forced   c. interested   d. encouraged

3. As the blind man walked through the courtyard, he grazed the wall.
   a. smelled   b. pushed   c. grabbed   d. touched lightly

4. The blind man was amused at the writer's questions.
   a. angry   b. unhappy   c. pleased   d. surprised

5. The blind man fumbled for the ticket.
   a. asked softly   b. asked loudly
   c. reached clumsily   d. reached delicately

B. Complete the sentences with words from the list.

initiative	grazed	dark
puzzle	pleased	pale
shade	amused	thin
light	surprised	

The writer was satisfied with himself because he had taken the

_____ to go up and down the tower. But then he was

_____ to see a blind man planning to climb up the tower. The

man was _____ and _____ and wore _____

glasses. He walked along the courtyard wall, _____ it with his

arm, and then he disappeared. To the writer, it was a _____
that a blind man would climb a tower for the view. When the writer
spoke to the blind man, the man assumed an _____
expression and told the writer that he enjoyed feeling the
_____ and the _____ of the sun. The explanation
_____ the writer.

Comprehension _____

1. Where did the writer first see the blind man?
✓ 2. Why was the writer surprised to see the blind man buying a ticket?
3. How did the attendant react to the writer's questions?
✓ 4. Why do you think the blind man had an amused expression when he answered the writer?
5. Why did the blind man go up the tower?
✓ 6. What does the last line of the story mean?

Wordwork _____

CONNECTING IDEAS

Combine the sentences into one sentence using *as soon as*. You may have to change nouns to pronouns. Study the example.

EXAMPLE

He entered the tower. He saw a ticket attendant.

> *As soon as he entered the tower, he saw a ticket attendant.*

1. He reached the door. He went inside and up the staircase.

_____

2. He got his ticket. He started to walk to the door.

_____

3. I gave the attendant 50 lira. The attendant gave me a ticket.

_____

4. I slowed down. I heard his steps on the stairs.

_____

5. I reached the first corner of the bell tower. I saw the blind man.

_____

6. The blind man felt the sunlight. The blind man passed the window.

Describing People

1. The blind man was a pale, thin man with sparse, black hair. Describe two people (a man and a woman) that you know who look different from the blind man. Follow the same pattern as the sentence above.

   a. _____

   _____

   b. _____

   _____

2. Go somewhere such as a street corner or a park and observe the people around you. Then describe two strangers that you see.

   a. _____

   _____

   b. _____

   _____

Tickets

1. Most of us have had experiences in getting tickets. Tell about a time when you wanted to get tickets for an event or a trip but you couldn't.

   _____

   _____

2. Tell about a time when you were pleasantly surprised because you were able to get some tickets that you wanted.

   _____

   _____

3. For what kind of an event would you wait in line overnight to get tickets? Compare your answers with those of other students.

_____

_____

Courtesy

The writer wanted to be courteous to someone he didn't know and he said, "Excuse me" when he started to talk to the blind man.

What would you say if you wanted to be courteous in these situations?

1. You are a guest at a party and you want to leave.

_____

_____

2. You are at a dinner party and you don't like the food being served.

_____

_____

3. You see a stranger who is wearing the exact item of clothing you have been looking for.

_____

_____

4. A police officer stops your car and tells you that you have been speeding, but you feel that you have not been.

_____

_____

5. You ask for directions but don't understand what you hear.

_____

_____

6. You are in a no-smoking area and someone next to you is smoking.

_____

_____

Light and Shade

Many words contrast with each other and are sometimes called opposites. Write the opposites for the words below.

1. open _____
2. clean _____
3. sunny _____
4. thin _____

5. slowly _____
6. strong _____
7. blind _____
8. empty _____

Suggestions for Discussion and Writing _____

1. Both the writer and the blind man climbed the tower. What was similar about their reasons for doing that?

2. What kind of person was the attendant?

√3. What is the point of the story?

4. The title of the story is "A Game of Light and Shade." Why did the writer use the word *game*?

5. Do you think that the narrator would have followed a blind woman?

6. If you were the ticket seller, would you let the blind man go up to the tower?

Independent Study _____

1. Read another story by Arturo Vivante and write a review of it.

2. Look up the following words and be prepared to describe the differences in meaning: *courtesy, politeness, manners, respect, graciousness.*

3. Who were Laura Dewey Bridgman and Helen Keller? Write a report about one or both of these women.

4. Look up *braille* in an encyclopedia or a reference book. Write a short report about it.

5. What are some of the causes of blindness?

3

My Mother's Memoirs

Russell Banks

Russell Banks (b. 1940) is a contemporary American writer of short stories and novels. He writes with sympathy about small-town life and hard-working people whose lives have been affected by violence, alcoholism, and emotional disasters. His most recent novel, *The Sweet Hereafter* (1991), is about a tragedy in a small town—a bus accident in which fourteen children die. The novel is about how the people of the town look for something to blame.

The following selection is taken from *Success Stories*. Earl, the narrator, who lives in New Hampshire, has been visiting his mother, who lives alone in a one-room apartment in San Diego.

PRE-READING QUESTIONS

1. What kind of stories do you like to hear or read? Why do you like them?

2. Why do people like to listen to and read stories?

3. Has anyone told you stories that you weren't interested in? Why did that person tell the stories?

As I was leaving my mother that morning to drive back to Los Angeles and then fly home to New Hampshire, where my brother and sister and all my mother's grandchildren live and where all but the last few years of my mother's past was lived, she told me a new story. We stood in the shade of palm trees in the parking lot outside her glass-and-metal building for a few minutes, and she said to me in a concerned way, "You know that restaurant, the Pancake House, where you took me for breakfast this morning?"

I said yes and checked the time and flipped my suitcase into the back seat of the rented car.

"Well, I always have breakfast there on Wednesdays, it's on the way to where I baby-sit on Wednesdays, and this week something funny happened there. I sat alone way in the back, where they have that long, curving booth, and I didn't notice until I was halfway through my breakfast that at the far end of the booth a man was sitting there. He was maybe your age, a young man, but dirty and shabby. Especially dirty, and so I just looked away and went on eating my eggs and toast.

"But then I noticed he was looking at me, as if he knew me and didn't quite dare talk to me. I smiled, because maybe I did know him. I know just about everybody in the neighborhood now. But he was a stranger. And dirty. And I could see that he had been drinking for days.

"So I smiled and said to him, 'You want help, mister, don't you?' He needed a shave, and his clothes were filthy and all ripped, and his hair was a mess. You know the type. But something pathetic about his eyes made me want to talk to him. But honestly, Earl, I couldn't. I just couldn't. He was so dirty and all.

"Anyhow, when I spoke to him, just that little bit, he sort of came out of his daze and sat up straight for a second, like he was afraid I was going to complain to the manger and have him thrown out of the restaurant. 'What did you say to me?' he asked. His voice was weak but he was trying to make it sound strong, so it came out kind of loud and broken. 'Nothing,' I said, and I turned away from him and quickly finished my breakfast and left.

"That afternoon, when I was walking back home from my baby-sitting job, I went into the restaurant to see if he was there, but he wasn't. And the next morning, Thursday, I walked all the way over there to check again, even though I never eat breakfast at the Pancake House on Thursdays, but he was gone then too. And

then yesterday, Friday, I went back a third time. But he was gone."
She lapsed into a thoughtful silence and looked at her hands.

"Was he there this morning?" I asked, thinking coincidence was somehow the point of the story.

"No," she said. "But I didn't expect him to be there this morning. I'd stopped looking for him by yesterday."

"Well, why'd you tell me the story, then? What's it about?"

"About? Why, I don't know. Nothing, I guess. I just felt sorry for the man, and then because I was afraid, I shut up and left him alone." She was still studying her tiny hands.

"That's natural," I said. "You shouldn't feel guilty for that," I said, and I put my arms around her.

She turned her face into my shoulder. "I know, I know. But still . . ." Her blue eyes filled, her son was leaving again, gone for another six months or a year, and who would she tell her stories to while he was gone? Who would listen?

Glossary

flipped threw

way in the back far in the back

the type the kind of person

Vocabulary

A. Find the word(s) closest in meaning to the underlined word. Circle the best answer.

1. The young man in the restaurant looked <u>filthy</u>.
    a. old   b. hungry   c. dirty   d. poor

2. The mother wanted to <u>check</u> the restaurant to see if the man was still there.
    a. call   b. walk over to   c. look at   d. leave

3. The man's appearance was a <u>mess.</u>
    a. without any order   b. surprise
    c. very neat   d. without any clothes

4. The mother finally <u>shut up</u> and left the man alone.
    a. stood up   b. stopped talking
    c. sat down   d. closed her notebook

5. At first the writer didn't realize the <u>point</u> of the story.
   a. the moment it began   b. an idea that means nothing
   c. the moment it ended   d. an idea that gives meaning

B. Complete the sentences with words from the list. Some words may be used more than once.

daze	pathetic	tell
coincidence	concerned	expected
mess	sorry	shut up
point		

After his mother left the restaurant, she felt _____ that she had _____ and left the _____ young man alone. She was so _____ that she returned to the restaurant in the afternoon. She _____ to see the young man sitting there in a _____ with his hair still a _____. But he was gone. When she told the story to her son, he couldn't get the _____ of the story. He thought it was going to be a story about a _____ but he didn't realize that his mother just wanted someone to _____ her stories to.

Comprehension

1. Was the grandmother living near her grandchildren? Where was her family?
2. Why do you think Earl's mother was living in California?
3. Where did the writer and his mother have breakfast?
4. Who did the mother notice in the Pancake House?
5. Why didn't the mother want to continue talking to the man?
6. What did the writer ask his mother about her story?
7. Why did the mother tell her son the story?
8. Did Earl understand why his mother told him the story? How do we know that?

Wordwork _____

CONNECTING IDEAS

Combine the sentences into one sentence using *as* or *where*. You may have to change some nouns in the second sentence to pronouns, and you may want to omit some words.

EXAMPLE

I threw my suitcase in the car. I noticed that the door was dented.

As I threw my suitcase in the car, I noticed that the door was dented.

1. I was leaving my mother to drive back to Los Angeles. My mother told me a new story.

   _____

2. I was eating my breakfast in the Pancake House. I saw a man sitting at the end of the booth.

   _____

3. I was eating in a restaurant. They serve pancakes in the restaurant.

   _____

4. The young man was sitting in a restaurant. An older woman smiled at the young man.

   _____

5. The woman returned to the restaurant. The woman had seen the young man in the restaurant a few days before.

   _____

6. The narrator was flying home to New Hampshire. The narrator's brother and sister live in New Hampshire.

   _____

7. The young man got up to leave. The young man whispered something to the woman.

   _____

Feeling Guilty

1. Earl's mother felt guilty because she didn't speak to the man in the restaurant. Describe a time when you felt guilty about not doing something.

   _____

   _____

   _____

2. Describe a time when you felt guilty because you did do something.

   _____

   _____

   _____

Complaining

The young man seemed afraid that Earl's mother was going to complain to the manager.

1. Have you ever complained about something in a public place (in a restaurant, a movie theater, an airline counter, etc.)? Describe what happened.

   _____

   _____

   _____

2. Has anyone ever complained to you about something you said or did?

   _____

   _____

   _____

3. Have you ever complained to someone about their habits?

   _____

   _____

   _____

4. Some stores and businesses have suggestion boxes where you can make a complaint (and offer a solution to the problem). If the school you are attending had a suggestion box, what would you complain about?

_____

_____

_____

Figure it Out

Below each statement, write the details from the story that prove that the statement is true.

1. The author's mother lives in California.

_____

2. The author's mother has not lived in California for a long time.

_____

3. The mother works.

_____

4. The author doesn't live in California.

_____

5. The mother may not have a car.

_____

6. The mother didn't have pancakes at the Pancake House.

_____

7. The mother was a small woman.

_____

Something Funny

The word *funny* has different meanings. If you don't know them, check in a dictionary.

1. What did the word *funny* mean in this story?

   _____

2. What is its other common meaning?

   _____

3. Illustrate each meaning by describing something that you thought was funny.

   a. _____

   _____

   b. _____

   _____

Suggestions for Discussion and Writing _____

1. Why are stories so popular in all cultures?
2. Parents and children nowadays live far from each other. What are some advantages and disadvantages of this situation?
3. The man in the restaurant looked so dirty and shabby that the mother didn't want to talk to him. Can you tell what people are like from the way they are dressed?
4. In what way is Earl's mother similar to the father in "The Last Escapade"? In what way is Earl similar to Keith?
5. Earl's mother thought the man in the restaurant had been drinking. What evidence do you think the mother had?
6. What are some ways of showing love without saying "I love you"?

Independent Study

1. Read another short story by Russell Banks and be ready to write or tell the class about it.

2. Suppose that the young man had been in the restaurant when the mother went back there. What do you think she would have said to him?

3. Look up these words and be prepared to describe the differences in meaning: *anxious, worried, nervous, concerned.*

4. Look up these words and be prepared to describe the differences in meaning: *filthy, shabby, offensive, grimy, untidy.*

5. Most stories have points. Choose a story that you have read and liked. Retell the story and explain what you think the main point of the story was.

6. Imagine you are in a restaurant and you notice a little old lady eating there alone. Write a paragraph about your concern for her.

Review

1. Which of the stories in this unit did you like best? Why?

2. Compare the stories of Vivante and Saroyan. In what ways are they similar? In what ways are they different?

3. Read the poems, "My Heart Leaps Up" and "Composed upon Westminster Bridge" by William Wordsworth. How are the feelings expressed in those poems similar to what you have read in this unit?

4. What do you think is the importance of art (painting, music, drama, etc.) today? Because of financial problems, many schools are offering fewer courses in the arts. Are these the wrong courses to eliminate?

5. Create a room that you think describes you. What treasures would you put in it? What colors would you use to decorate?

6. Find a poem or story that describes light or color. For example, read the poem "The Customer" by Amy Lowell. How many different colors of red were mentioned?

UNIT SIX
Milestones

UNIT INTRODUCTION

The stories selected for this unit have to do with milestones, important moments in the lives of people, usually when something happens to influence the direction of their lives. In this excerpt from *Tell Me That You Love Me Junie Moon* three people with very serious physical problems decide to try to live together. In "Popular Mechanics," a couple decides to divorce, and in this reflection from the novel, *Jack*, a boy realizes that his father is gay.

UNIT PRE-READING

1. What are usually the most important moments of our lives?

2. Has there been a time when you did something or decided something that changed the direction of your life?

3. What is one of the most important decisions you have made?

4. Do you agree with the saying that "beauty is only skin deep"?

1

Tell Me That You Love Me, Junie Moon

Marjorie Kellogg

Marjorie Kellogg (b. 1922) is an American writer who grew up in rural California and worked as a hospital social worker. She has written a number of plays for television and for the theater. *Tell Me That You Love Me, Junie Moon* was her first novel. Many critics have called it beautiful and touching. Kellogg writes with humor and understanding, often about people who have serious physical or mental problems. She is good at creating characters that the reader does not forget easily. Her personal philosophy is that "art, like love, will survive all the abuse man can give it."

In the first chapter of the book, Kellogg describes how Junie, Warren, and Arthur decide to live together.

PRE-READING QUESTIONS

1. Do you know any people with serious physical problems? What are their problems? What kinds of things can they do or not do?

2. Do you know any people with serious physical problems who live by themselves? If so, how are they able to do it?

3. Why do you think that many people object to the word "freaks"?

4. Communities often object to having special housing in their neighborhoods. Why do you think this is so?

Once there were three patients who met in the hospital and decided to live together. They arrived at this decision because they had no place to go when they were discharged.

Despite the fact that these patients often quarreled and nagged each other, and had, so far as they knew, nothing in common, they formed an odd balance—like three pawnshop balls.

The first patient was called Warren. When he was seventeen, he and a friend were out hunting rabbits when the friend's gun went off and the bullet struck Warren in the middle of his spine. From then on he was paraplegic and spent the rest of his days in a wheelchair.

The second patient was Arthur. He had a progressive neurological disease which no one had been able to diagnose. He estimated that he had been asked to touch his finger to his nose 6,012 times, and he could recite the laboratory findings on himself for the past five years, in case the doctors wanted them reviewed. Arthur walked with a careening gait and his hands fluttered about his face like butterflies.

The third patient was a woman named Junie Moon. That was her real name. An irate man had beaten her half to death in an alley one night and had topped off his violence by throwing acid over her. She had a number of pitiful and pesky deformities.

The idea of their living together originated with Warren. He was fat and lazy and did not relish the thought of being alone or looking after himself. He was also a cheerful organizer of other people's time and affairs and could paint lovely pictures of how things would be later on.

"My dear friends," he said to Arthur and Junie Moon one night after the evening medications had been given out, "I have a solution to our collective dilemma." Junie Moon, who was playing checkers with Arthur in the far end of the corridor, scowled at Warren from her torn, disfigured face.

"With the various pittances we could collect from this and that source," Warren went on, as Arthur inadvertently knocked two checkers on the floor, "we could live fairly comfortably." Warren retrieved the checkers and patted Arthur on the shoulder. "What do you think?"

"Nobody wants to live with me," Junie Moon said, "so shut up about it."

"I think the idea stinks," Arthur said, as his hand flew into the air.

Then he and Junie Moon bent closer to the board as if to dismiss Warren's preposterous scheme.

"Don't pretend that either of you have a place to go," Warren said, leaning forward in his wheelchair so that his face was on a level with theirs, "because you haven't!" He gave Junie Moon a lascivious wink: "You'll end up at the old-ladies home and you know what goes on *there*!"

"At least it's better than nothing," she said. Her scarred mouth shifted painfully to permit a laugh. Warren was still not used to her face, but he loved her quick humor.

"But I'm better than a dozen old ladies," he said, "and more responsible."

"Baloney!" shouted Arthur, which set off a terrible spasm of his body and almost lifted him from his chair. Automatically, Warren and Junie Moon laid a hand on his shoulders to quiet him.

"You are many things," Arthur said when he had regained control of himself, "but responsible is not one of them."

"But he may be better than the poorhouse at that," Junie Moon said. "What do you have in mind?"

"Well now!" Warren reared back in his wheelchair and stroked his bright blond beard. He said: "We will each have our own room. Junie Moon will do the cooking. Arthur will go to the store. I can see it all now."

"And I can see you have planned nothing for yourself in the way of expended effort," Arthur said.

"Who in their right mind would rent us an apartment?" Junie Moon said. "Three freaks, one a female."

"We'll do it by phone," Warren said. "We'll say we're much too busy to come in person."

"When the landlord takes one look at us, he will throw us out," Junie Moon said.

"He couldn't," Arthur said. "We represent at least three different minority groups." By making this remark, Arthur had cast his vote in favor of the plan. Junie Moon held out a little longer.

"It's bad enough seeing the two of you in this hospital every day," she said, "let alone living with you."

At this, the men banded together and attacked her.

"You're no prize yourself," Warren said.

"And you probably have a lot of disgusting personal habits of which we are not aware and to which you will expose us once we agree to a common arrangement," Arthur said.

"Let's not talk about prizes," Junie Moon said to Warren. "If we did, you might take the cake."

Arthur, who was the more sensitive of the two men, realized by something in Junie Moon's voice that they had hurt her feelings. Because her face was so disfigured, it was difficult to read her emotions.

"I suppose none of us would take a prize," Arthur said. "On the other hand, we have a few things in our favor, I believe." He turned his head abruptly so the other two could not see him blush over this self-compliment.

"What are you three up to?" Miss Oxford, the chief nurse, asked, looking thin and suspicious.

"We are plotting your demise," Warren said, cheerfully. Miss Oxford scurried away, glancing over her shoulder.

Junie Moon then decided to join the two men in their plan. "I've thought of a number of ways to get that nurse," she said. "We must try a few of them before we leave here to set up housekeeping."

That was the way they decided.

Glossary

went off   fired

topped off   completed

looking after   taking care of

Baloney!   an expression of disbelief

in their right mind   thinking normally

held out   resisted

take the cake   win the prize, be the best

up to   planning

to get   attack, get revenge

Vocabulary

A. Find the word(s) closest in meaning to the underlined word. Circle the best answer.

1. Even though they <u>nagged</u> each other, they were friends.
   a. laughed at   b. bothered   c. talked about   d. hit

2. None of them would <u>relish</u> the idea of living alone.
   a. regain   b. enjoy   c. give up   d. think of

3. At first, Warren's plan seemed <u>preposterous</u> to Junie and Arthur.
   a. clever   b. lascivious   c. disgusting   d. senseless

4. They were afraid that the people outside the hospital would consider them <u>freaks.</u>
   a. very poor people   b. very sick people
   c. very strange people   d. very unintelligent people

5. The three of them together seemed to create an <u>odd</u> balance.
   a. strange   b. unhealthy   c. happy   d. disgusting

B. Complete the sentences with words from the list.

balance	originated	irate	flutter
spasms	disfigured	cheerful	diagnose
	discharged	sensitive	neurological

Junie Moon's face was _____ by an _____ boy

friend, but she remained _____ with a good sense of humor.

Arthur's problem was _____. He had _____ and his

hands would _____, but the doctors couldn't seem to

_____ it exactly. On the other hand, Warren's condition

_____ in a physical act. Someone shot him. The three patients

were _____. Their dilemma was that they were going to be

_____ by the hospital and they had no place to go.

Comprehension

1. Why did the three patients have to decide what to do?
2. What had happened to Warren?
3. Why was Junie Moon deformed?
4. Why did Warren want them to live together?
5. How did Junie and Arthur react to Warren's idea at first?
6. What was Warren's plan for who would cook and shop?
7. Why was Junie worried that they wouldn't be able to rent an apartment?
8. What was the attitude of the three patients toward each other?

Wordwork

CONNECTING IDEAS

Combine the sentences into one sentence using *of which, with which,* or *about which.* You may have to change the order of the sentences.

EXAMPLE

They had plans. We were not told about their plans.

They had plans about which we were not told.

1. You have bad habits. We were not aware of your bad habits.

2. She had a sense of humor. She amused Warren with her sense of humor.

3. Junie had a disfigured face. She was sensitive about her disfigured face.

4. Warren had a wheelchair. He moved around with a wheelchair.

5. The three of them had a plan. The nurse knew nothing about their plan.

   _____

6. You have a lot of disgusting personal habits. You will expose us to your disgusting personal habits.

   _____

Despite the Fact That . . .

Combine the sentences into one sentence using *despite the fact that.* You may have to change some nouns to pronouns, as well as the order of the sentences.

EXAMPLE

People in the outside world might consider them freaks. The patients decided to leave the hospital.

> *The patients decided to leave the hospital despite the fact*
>
> *that people in the outside world might consider them freaks.*

1. The patients often quarreled with each other. The patients decided to live together.

   _____

   _____

2. They had enough money to rent an apartment. No one would rent them an apartment.

   _____

   _____

3. The patients criticized each other. The patients were friends.

   _____

   _____

4. Junie said that she didn't like seeing Warren and Arthur every day. Junie decided to live with Warren and Arthur.

_____

_____

5. Arthur had gone to many doctors. The doctors couldn't diagnose Arthur's illness.

_____

_____

6. Arthur thought that Warren was not responsible. Arthur voted in favor of the plan.

_____

_____

Nobody Wants To . . .

Complete the sentences below with things that nobody wants to see, hear, think about, etc.

1. Nobody wants to see _____.

2. Nobody wants to hear _____.

3. Nobody wants to think about _____.

4. Nobody wants to _____.

5. Nobody wants to _____.

Compare your answers with those of other students.

That's Preposterous

We call something *preposterous* when we think it is absolutely impossible. Create a dialogue from history or from nowadays about something that seemed or seems preposterous.

EXAMPLE

_____ *Columbus: I'm going to sail west and get to Asia.*

_____ *King Ferdinand: My Advisors say that's preposterous.*

_____

_____

Tell Me That You Love Me, Junie Moon **169**

Used To

"Warren was not used to Junie's face." Make sure that you know the meaning of *used to* here.

1. Describe something that you are not used to at the present time.

   _____

   _____

2. Ask other students what they are not used to and compare answers. What's the most common answer?

   _____

   _____

Paint a Picture

Warren "could paint a lovely picture of how things would be later on."

1. What details did Warren tell the other two to convince them to live together?

   _____

   _____

2. Describe "a lovely picture" that you painted to convince someone of something. Include the details that you used.

   _____

   _____

Suggestions for Discussion and Writing _____

1. Junie Moon described living together as "better than nothing." What does that mean? What are some other situations that you would describe as better than nothing?

2. Where do you think people like Warren, Arthur and Junie, should live if they have no friends or family? What happens to people like that in your country?

3. Which person do you have the most sympathy for? Why?

4. Imagine that you have to live in a wheelchair. What would be the most difficult things for you to do?

5. If you were a landlord, what kinds of people would you refuse to rent to? If you were a landlord, would you object to renting to a person with a neurological disease?

6. How do you think the neighbors react when they see Warren, Arthur and Junie moving into their house?

Independent Study _____

1. Look up the meanings of these words and be prepared to describe the differences in meaning: *quarrel, nag, argue, squabble, sulk.*

2. This story begins with the words "Once there were . . ." Many fables being like that in English. Look up the word *fable* and then tell why you think the author might begin this story like that.

3. Sometimes people use difficult words instead of simple words to be funny. Warren does that in this story. Make a list of some difficult words you found in this story and next to them write simpler words with similar meanings.

4. Read all of *Tell Me That You Love Me, Junie Moon.* Describe Sidney Wyner. What would you do if he were your neighbor?

5. Find out what kinds of accommodations are made for handicapped students at your school.

6. What is the Americans with Disabilities Act? What are some of its provisions?

2
Popular Mechanics

Raymond Carver

Raymond Carver (1938–1988) won many awards and honors for his poetry, creative writing, and short stories. Many of his short stories are about ordinary people, unsatisfactory relationships, and loneliness. The language in his stories is the language of ordinary people struggling to survive. "Popular Mechanics" is from Carver's third collection of short stories called *What We Talk About When We Talk About Love.*

PRE-READING QUESTIONS

1. Think of people you know who are not happy in their marriage. Why are they unhappy?

2. Do you know any children whose parents are divorced? How do the children feel about the situation? Was it the fighting before the break-up that caused the most pain?

3. Have your parents ever fought over you? Which parent takes your side most frequently?

4. Do you know anyone who has been involved in a custody case?

Early that day the weather turned and the snow was melting into dirty water. Streaks of it ran down from the little shoulder-high window that faced the backyard. Cars slushed by on the street outside, where it was getting dark. But it was getting dark on the inside too.

He was in the bedroom pushing clothes into a suitcase when she came to the door.

I'm glad you're leaving! I'm glad you're leaving! she said. Do you hear?

He kept on putting his things into the suitcase.

Son of a bitch! I'm so glad you're leaving! She began to cry. You can't even look me in the face, can you?

Then she noticed the baby's picture on the bed and picked it up.

He looked at her and she wiped her eyes and stared at him before turning and going back to the living room.

Bring that back, he said.

Just get your things and get out, she said.

He did not answer. He fastened the suitcase, put on his coat, looked around the bedroom before turning off the light. Then he went out to the living room.

She stood in the doorway of the little kitchen, holding the baby.

I want the baby, he said.

Are you crazy?

No, but I want the baby. I'll get someone to come by for his things.

You're not touching this baby, she said.

The baby had begun to cry and she uncovered the blanket from around his head.

Oh, oh, she said, looking at the baby.

He moved toward her.

For God's sake! she said. She took a step back into the kitchen.

I want the baby.

Get out of here!

She turned and tried to hold the baby over in a corner behind the stove.

But he came up. He reached across the stove and tightened his hands on the baby.

Let go of him, he said.

Get away, get away! she cried.

The baby was red-faced and screaming. In the scuffle they knocked down a flowerpot that hung behind the stove.

He crowded her into the wall then, trying to break her grip. He held on to the baby and pushed with all his weight.

Let go of him, he said.

Don't she said. You're hurting the baby, she said.

I'm not hurting the baby, he said.

The kitchen window gave no light. In the near-dark he worked on her fisted fingers with one hand and with the other hand he gripped the screaming baby up under an arm near the shoulder.

She felt her fingers being forced open. She felt the baby going from her.

No! she screamed just as her hands came loose.

She would have it, this baby. She grabbed for the baby's other arm. She caught the baby around the wrist and leaned back.

But he would not let go. He felt the baby slipping out of his hands and he pulled back very hard.

In this manner, the issue was decided.

Glossary

turned changed

son of a bitch swear words

Vocabulary _____

A. Find the word(s) closest in meaning to the underlined words. Circle the best answer.

1. He <u>kept on</u> putting his things into a suitcase.
   a. stopped   b. began   c. continued   d. held back

2. I want you to <u>get out of</u> here.
   a. sit   b. come back   c. stay   d. leave

3. He <u>gripped</u> the baby under the arm.
   a. scratched   b. touched   c. threw   d. held

4. They had a <u>scuffle</u> in the kitchen.
   a. supper   b. fight   c. argument   d. suitcase

5. They decided the <u>issue</u> by fighting over the baby.
   a. important point   b. unimportant point
   c. marriage   d. child

B. Complete the sentences with the words from the list. A few words must be used more than once.

put on	picked up	held on
let go	turned off	kept on
get out		

After he _____ the suitcase, he _____ the light,

_____ his coat, and went into the living room. She

_____ the baby and held it. When he said that he wanted the

baby, she told him to _____. But he grabbed the baby and told

her to _____ of it. She wouldn't; she _____ to the

baby. He _____ pushing and pulling and, although she caught

the baby around the wrist, he wouldn't _____.

Comprehension

1. What was the weather like?
2. Why did the writer say it was getting dark?
3. Who was leaving the house?
4. What did the woman think about the man's leaving?
5. Who wanted the baby?
6. How did they decide who would have the baby?

Wordwork

CONNECTING IDEAS

Combine the sentences into one sentence. Use the appropriate connectives.

EXAMPLE

He was in the bedroom. He was pushing clothes into a suitcase. She came to the door.

> *He was in the bedroom pushing clothes*
>
> *into a suitcase when she came to the door.*

1. He looked at her. She wiped her eyes. She stared at him.

2. He put on his coat. He looked around the bedroom. He turned off the light.

3. The baby began to cry. She uncovered the blanket from the baby's head.

_____

_____

4. They knocked down a flowerpot. The flowerpot hung behind the stove.

_____

_____

5. He crowded her into the wall. He was trying to break her grip.

_____

_____

6. She held on to the baby. He gripped the baby. He pushed with all his weight.

_____

_____

7. He felt the baby slipping out of his hands. He pulled back very hard.

_____

_____

Command

There are several command sentences in this story since the man and the woman are angry at each other. For each of the situations below, write an appropriate command.

EXAMPLE

She wanted her husband to leave the house immediately.

_____ _Get out of the house right now!_ _____

1. Your roommate is asleep and there is a fire in the room.

_____

2. You are outside and a ball is coming toward your friend's head.

_____

3. You are going to the bank with a friend. It is five minutes before four and the bank closes at four, but your friend is walking very slowly.

_____

4. Your friends are leaving to go to the movies and you decide to go with them.

_____

Prepositions

Complete the sentences with a preposition. There may be two or three possible choices for each sentence.

1. She looked _____ the baby.

2. He turned _____ the light.

3. She looked _____ the bedroom.

4. He stood _____ the kitchen.

5. She walked _____ the living room.

6. He reached _____ the stove.

7. The flowerpot was hanging _____ the stove.

8. He was putting his things _____ the suitcase.

9. I'll send someone to come _____ the baby's things.

Nouns and Verbs

Many words in English can be both nouns and verbs. For each word below, write two sentences. In one sentence, use the word as a noun; in the other sentence, use it as a verb.

EXAMPLE

hand   *She held the baby by the hand.*

        She did not want to hand the baby to him.

1. snow _____

_____

2. cry _____

_____

3. step _____

_____

4. scream _____

_____

5. crowd _____

_____

6. grip _____

_____

Arguments

People can argue about many things. For each situation below, write a sentence that describes what they *might argue about.*

EXAMPLE

A couple getting a divorce

They might argue about the children.

1. Roomates with one T.V. set.

_____

2. A couple on their first date.

_____

3. Two opposing sports teams.

_____

4. A teacher and a student

_____

5. A coach and a referee

_____

6. A policeofficer and the driver of a car

_____

7. A mother and a child in a supermarket

_____

8. A couple on their last date

_____

Suggestions for Discussion and Writing _____

1. Imagine why the couple in the story might be having problems.
2. What are some of the reasons why people divorce?
3. What are some of the reasons why people get married? Are some reasons better than others?
4. The man seems to be winning the fight because he is using force. Is this acceptable?
5. If you were the woman in this story, what would you do?
6. What do you think the title of the story means?

Independent Study

1. Look up the following words and be prepared to describe the differences in meaning: *fight, battle, scuffle, quarrel.*
2. Read another short story by Raymond Carver and be prepared to tell it to the class.
3. Describe the attitude toward divorce in your country. What happens when people are unhappy in their marriages?
4. Go to the library and look up "battered woman syndrome" in a periodical index. Read an article about it in a magazine and summarize it for the class.
5. If the father in the story took his baby to the hospital because its arm was hurt, what would the hospital do?
6. Go to the library and find out what are the most common instances of child abuse.

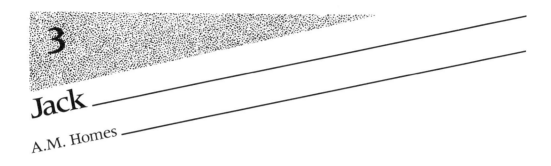

Jack

A.M. Homes

A.M. Homes (b. 1959) attended Sarah Lawrence College and the University of Iowa Writers Workshop and has received a number of writing awards. In addition to the novel *Jack*, she has written a collection of ten short stories entitled *The Safety of Objects*.

Jack is an amusing yet serious story of a fifteen-year-old boy who lives in the suburbs. His parents are separated, but he has a best friend and he thinks his life is normal. He wants his life to be normal and happy, but one day his father tells him something that changes his life. In the following selection, Jack's father has invited Jack to go rowing with him on a lake.

PRE-READING QUESTIONS

1. What kinds of difficulties are faced by homosexuals? What kinds of problems do their families have?

2. What are some of the attitudes toward homosexuals in your culture?

3. What stereotypes about homosexuals are the most distressing?

When he finished counting the life preservers and checking the boat for leaks, he let me get in and then rowed us out to the middle of the lake.

As soon as we were out in the middle of nothing, he started getting the look fathers get when they're about to say something they know is gonna make you lose your lunch. It's a classic thing. Their eyebrows bunch together, and then they lean forward and say something like, Son, we need to talk. Then they pause for about half an hour and you practically have a heart attack while you're waiting. Finally, they say something like, Your grandmother's very ill, which usually means she's already dead but they're saving that for tomorrow.

This time it was even worse because he wasn't talking about someone being sick or anything like that. He was trying to tell me something about himself. He stopped rowing.

"Jack," he said. "I need to talk to you."

I nodded.

"I've been spending a lot of time trying to figure things out."

His voice was cracking all over the place.

"It's not an excuse. And I don't know if you're going to understand what I have to tell you."

He reached out and grabbed my arm. I pulled away. It wasn't as if I meant to; it just happened, like I was on autopilot or something.

"Jack, what I'm trying to say is that all these years, even back before you were born, I've been running away from myself, and a person can't do that forever. It begins to catch up."

I sat there staring down at the broken oarlocks, trying to figure out what the hell he was talking about. The green paint on the boat was chipping and a sort of punk fluorescent orange poked through.

"What?" I said.

"I realized . . ." He paused. "I'd be happier if I didn't live with your mother."

"I thought that was awhile ago."

He wasn't listening.

"I love her," he said. "I always will. But I'm happy now, living with another man."

I must have given him a pretty funny look at that point, but I don't think I realized what he was saying.

"Jack, I've fallen in love with another man."

He stopped for a second and drew in his breath.

"You know Bob?" he asked.

Bob was his old friend, a guy he'd just rented an apartment with.

"Bob, the guy we went on that trip with, the guy who's your roommate now?"

He gave me a funny look, a very funny look. It didn't make sense.

"Bob and I, we sleep together."

I cut him off. "What are you talking about?"

"We're lovers." He blurted it out, an explosion like a firecracker.

I looked out at the water. Dragonflies were hovering over the scum. I wanted to get up, to run, but thanks to my dad, we were in the middle of a goddamned lake. I thought I was going to throw up. I could taste it in the back of my mouth.

"I'm sick," I said.

My father leaned into the oars and rowed to the dock. I jumped out and started running. After about a quarter mile, I slowed down to a walk. I'm not a goddamned marathon runner.

My dad was in the car behind me, but I didn't turn around. He passed me and stopped.

"Get in, I'll give you a ride."

"I'll walk," I said.

He took his foot off the brake and coasted next to me.

"Jack, I'm your father. I love you."

"Get away," I said.

"Don't act this way. Don't do this to me."

"Do what?" I yelled. "You're the one who did it."

I walked faster, but he kept the car at my side. From the corner of my eye I could see him steering with one hand and leaning out the window to talk to me.

"Jack, I told you. I didn't have to, but I thought you should know. It's okay. It doesn't have to change anything. You're my boy, my son."

I walked the whole way home with him trailing behind me like a lost dog. I went up the front steps into the house. My mom was sitting in the kitchen talking to her friend Elaine—Max's mom—on the phone.

"Jack?" she said when I slammed the door.

"Don't bother."

"They're back," she said to Elaine. "I'll call you later."

"Go ahead, talk to her now. Tell her the whole story. I'm sure you will, if you haven't already."

I ran up the steps to my room. From my window I could see my father parked in the middle of the street, hanging out the window of the goddamned car.

I stayed in my room all night, trying to figure out how my father could be queer. I mean, historically, queers are not fathers.

Glossary

gonna   going to

lose your lunch   throw up, vomit

classic   typical

practically   almost

what the hell   slang for "what"

punk   a style of music and clothes

funny   strange

cut him off   interrupted him

goddamned   damned

queer   homosexual

Vocabulary

A. Find the word(s) closest in meaning to the underlined word(s). Circle the best answer.

1. Jack was trying to figure out what had happened to his father.
   a. believe   b. say   c. hear   d. understand

2. When he got home, he slammed the front door.
   a. knocked on   b. opened with force
   c. broke   d. closed with force

3. Jack's father paused before he told Jack the truth.
   a. stopped for a long time   b. began again
   c. stopped for a short time   d. finished

4. Jack couldn't talk to his father, but he nodded.
   a. cried   b. moved his head up and down
   c. moved his head sideways   d. raised his hand

5. His father decided to <u>check</u> the boat before they got in.
   a. pay for   b. clean up   c. practice with   d. examine

B. Complete the sentences with the words from the list.

slammed	ran	fallen in love
needed	rowed	throw up
paused	blurted out	figure out
stared	jumped out	
nodded		

After his father _____ the boat to the middle of the lake,

he told Jack that he _____ to talk to him. Jack didn't say

anything; he just _____. His father _____ and then

_____ the truth, "I've _____ with another man." Jack

_____ at him, he couldn't believe it. He felt as if he were

going to _____.

When his father rowed back to shore, Jack _____ of the

boat and started running home. When he got there, he _____

the front door and _____ to his room. He thought about the

situation for awhile and couldn't _____ how his father had

changed.

Comprehension

1. How did Jack know that his father was going to tell him something important?
2. What did the father mean when he said that he had been running away from himself?
3. What did the father say about his life with Jack's mother?
4. What was the father's important news?
5. What did Jack say when his father told him about Bob?
6. What did Jack do?
7. What relationship did his father want with Jack?
8. At the end of the selection, what is it that is puzzling Jack?

9. At the beginning of the selection, the author describes Jack's father checking the boat. What does that tell us about the father?

Wordwork _____

CONNECTING THE IDEAS

Combine the sentences into one sentence using *as soon as*. You may have to change the order of the sentences. Make sure that your new sentences are true to what happens in the story.

EXAMPLE

My father finished checking the boat for leaks. He let me get into the boat.

> *As soon as my father finished checking the boat*
>
> *for leaks, he let me get into the boat.*

1. My father started getting a certain look. We were out in the middle of the lake.

   _____

2. He reached out and grabbed my arm. I pulled it away.

   _____

3. I cut him off. He said that he was sleeping with Bob.

   _____

4. I jumped out and started running. The boat reached the dock.

   _____

5. I slammed the door. My mother said, "Jack?"

   _____

Gonna Go

The author tries to make Jack's speech sound more natural by writing words such as *gonna*, which is the way Jack might have said *going to*. For the spoken forms listed below, write the written forms and use them in sentences that Jack or his father could have spoken.

Jack **187**

EXAMPLE

gonna: *going to—Jack knew his father was going to say something important.*

1. wanna: _____

2. gotta: _____

3. didja: _____

4. waddya: _____

5. hadda: _____

Would Be Happier If

Complete the sentences below with your own ideas.

1. Jack would be happier if _____

2. I'd be happier if _____

3. Would you be happier if _____

4. Why would Jack be happier if _____

5. They'd be happier if _____

It Doesn't Make Sense

Tell about two things that someone said or did that didn't make sense to you. Explain why it didn't make sense.

1. _____

_____

_____

2. _____

_____

_____

Bad News

How would you tell someone bad news?

1. What would you say if you borrowed a friend's car and you damaged it?

_____

2. How would you tell your parent(s) or relatives that you failed a course in school?

_____

3. How would you tell a boy or girlfriend that you don't want to go out with them anymore?

_____

4. What would you say to your neighbors if you threw a ball through the window of their house?

_____

5. How would you tell a friend that you ran over his cat?

_____

6. How would you tell your best friend that your parents were getting a divorce?

_____

Compare your answers with those of other students.

Compare

Complete the sentences below using a comparison.

EXAMPLE

My father was trailing behind me like a lost dog.

1. The car was going as slowly as _____

2. I can run as fast as _____

3. The room was as quiet as _____

4. The room was noisy like _____

5. His voice exploded like _____

6. When I heard my father's news, I felt as if _____

7. She looked as if _____

8. The damaged truck looked as if _____

Suggestions for Discussion and Writing

1. How do you think Jack's friends will react when they hear about his father?

2. What do you think will happen to Jack's relationship with his father?

3. What are some of the problems for the children of parents who are separated?

4. How do you think Jack would react if he found out that his mother was gay?

5. Jack wants to be normal. Do you think his reaction to his father's news was normal? How do you think you would react to such news?

6. What problems do gay high-school students have?

7. Define the word "family."

Independent Study

1. Look up the following words and be prepared to describe the differences in meaning: *check, revise, review, examine.*

2. Look up the following words and be prepared to describe the differences in meaning: *vomit, burp, hiccough, spit, sweat.*

3. Find out what these words mean: *gay, come out of the closet, lesbian, faggot, straight.*

4. Go to the library and look up "gay rights." Read an article from a newspaper or periodical and be prepared to report on it to the class.

5. Read the novel *Jack* and find out what happened to Jack at the end of the novel.

6. Some current research indicates that homosexuals are born that way. Read an article that supports or does not support that research.

7. Do you think that children of homosexuals grow up to be homosexual? Go to the library and find an article that supports or does not support your belief.

8. *Now That You Know* by Norma Klein is a novel with a similar theme. You might want to read it and compare both stories.

Review

1. Which one of the characters in this unit would you feel most comfortable with? Which one of the characters described in this unit would you most like to have as a friend?

2. Both Jack and the baby in "Popular Mechanics" are children of parents who are separated. Which one do you think will grow up to be the least secure? Which one do you think will be the most successful?

3. This unit deals with milestones, important moments in the lives of people. What other topics could have been included in this unit?

4. Do you think Arthur and Warren would make good fathers? Would they be better fathers than Jack's father? Would they be better fathers than the father in "Popular Mechanics"?

5. Would Junie Moon make a good mother? Would she be a better mother than the mother in "Popular Mechanics"? Do you think Jack's mother is a good mother?

6. If a family is a "group of individuals living under one roof," are Junie, Arthur, and Warren a family? Is Jack's father and Bob a family?

7. In each story in this unit, the characters decide to change their living arrangements. Which decision required the most courage? Who made the worse decision?

PAGE 74 – PUZZLES AND MYSTERIES

1. He juggled them as he went across.

2. a. He took the goat over.
   b. He took the wolf over and he took the goat back.
   c. He took the cabbage over (leaving the goat behind).
   d. He went back and got the goat.

   or

   a. He took the goat over.
   b. He took the cabbage over and he took the goat back.
   c. He took the wolf over (leaving the goat behind).
   d. He went back and got the goat.

PAGE 74 – INDEPENDENT STUDY

1. Evans was right. The police couldn't arrest him for murder. But Evans had forgotten that he had planned the murder in New York with the help of a friend. Planning a murder, which is a form of conspiracy, is also a serious crime. Therefore, when the plane landed, the police arrested Evans and sent him back to New York where he had committed the crime of conspiracy.

ACKNOWLEDGEMENTS

Page 45 from "Significant Moments in the Life of My Mother," in BLUE-BEARD'S EGG by Margaret Atwood. Copyright (c) 1983, 1986 by O.W. Toad, Ltd. First American Edition 1986. Reprinted by permission of Houghton Mifflin Company, Jonathan Cape Ltd., and the Canadian publishers, McClelland & Stewart, Toronto. All rights reserved. Page 151 from "My Mother's Memoirs" in SUCCESS STORIES by Russell Banks. Copyright (c) 1986 by Russell Banks. Reprinted by permission of Russell Banks and HarperCollins Publishers. Page 173 "Popular Mechanics" from WHAT WE TALK ABOUT WHEN WE TALK ABOUT LOVE by Raymond Carver. Copyright (c) 1981 Raymond Carver and Tess Gallagher. Reprinted by permission of Alfred A. Knopf, Inc. and Tess Gallagher. Page 67 from "A Case for the UN" by Miriam Allen de Ford, in ELLERY QUEEN MYSTERY MAGAZINE (1964). Page 35 from "Mother Dear and Daddy" in BEYOND THE ANGRY BLACK by Junius Edwards. Copyright (c) 1966. Page 97 "How My Love Was Sawed in Half" by Robert Fontaine. Copyright (c) 1960 by The Atlantic. Reprinted with permission. Page 119 from "Jones Beach" in WINDSONG by Nicholas Gagarin. Copyright (c) 1970 by Nicholas Gagarin. Reprinted by permission of William Morrow and Company and John Hawkins & Associates. Page 3 from "The Oyster" in MOOLTIKI: STORIES AND POEMS FROM INDIA by Rumer Godden. Copyright © 1957 by Rumer Godden. Reprinted by permission of Curtis Brown Ltd., Page 183 from JACK by A.M. Homes. Reprinted with the permission of Macmillan Publishing Company and Donadio & Ashworth Inc. Copyright 1989 A.M. Homes. Page 163 excerpt from TELL ME THAT YOU LOVE ME, JUNIE MOON by Marjorie Kellogg. Copyright (c) 1968 by Marjorie Kellogg. Reprinted by permission of Farrar, Straus & Giroux, Inc. and Martin Secker & Warburg. Page 21 excerpts from LUCY by Jamaica Kincaid. Copyright (c) 1990 by Jamaica Kincaid. Reprinted by permission of Farrar, Straus & Giroux, Inc. and Wylie, Aitken & Stone, Inc. Page 77 "Drum Beat" by Stephen Marlowe reprinted by permission of the author and the author's agents, Scott Meredith Literary Agency, Inc., 845 Third Avenue, New York, NY 10022. Page 87 "Death Speaks" from "An Appointment in Samarra," in SHEPPEY by W. Somerset Maugham. Copyright 1933 by W. Somerset Maugham. Used by permission of Doubleday, a division of Bantam Doubleday Dell Publishing Group, Inc. and A.P. Watt Ltd. on behalf of The Royal Literary Fund. Page 55 "The Last Escapade" from Harry Mark Petrakis, THE COLLECTED STORIES copyright 1987 by Harry Mark Petrakis. Reprinted by permission from Lake View Press, Chicago. Page 107 "Estelle" from ANDOSHEN, PA by Darryl